Readers and texts
in the primary years

RETHINKING READING

Series Editor: Professor L. John Chapman

Readers and texts in the primary years

TONY MARTIN AND BOB LEATHER

Open University Press
Buckingham · Philadelphia

Open University Press
Celtic Court
22 Ballmoor
Buckingham
MK18 1XW

and

1900 Frost Road, Suite 101
Bristol, PA 19007, USA

First Published 1994

A catalogue record of this book is available from the British Library

ISBN   0 335 19227 0 (pb)   0 335 19228 9 (hb)

Library of Congress Cataloging-in-Publication Data

Martin, Tony, 1947–
    Readers and texts in the primary years/Tony Martin & Bob
Leather.
        p.   cm. – (Rethinking reading)
    Includes bibliographical references and index.
    ISBN 0–335–19228–9 (hb). – ISBN 0–335–19227–0 (pb)
    1. Reading (Elementary)   2. English literature–Study and teaching
(Elementary)   3. Reader-response criticism.   4. Children–Books and
reading.   I. Leather, Bob, 1941–   .   II. Title.   III. Series.
LB1573.M335 1994
372.4–dc20   94–12241
                                                                  CIP

Typeset by Dorwyn Ltd, Rowlands Castle, Hants
Printed in Great Britain by St Edmundsbury Press Ltd,
Bury St Edmunds, Suffolk

Contents

Acknowledgements

We would like to thank all of the child and adult readers who allowed us to share their responses to the stories, novels, poems and advertisements. In particular, we must mention the Low Nook readers, the Dove Cottage readers, the Charlotte Mason students, the groups at Castle Park Primary School and Y6 at Calthwaite C.E. School. Thanks also to Jan Horne, head-teacher of Calthwaite School, Wendy Yates at Coniston School (for George's story), Colette Hodgkison (for the video of Dominic and his father) and Kath Langley (for managing to transcribe a story while bathing her son). Tony would also like to acknowledge the enthusiasm of Emrys Evans who introduced him to Iser, and Bob Bibby for the time they worked on 'Do I Have to Read It?'.

Material used in Chapter 3 was presented at the 7th European and 28th UKRA Annual Conference at Heriot-Watt University, Edinburgh in July 1991 and appeared in the conference proceedings, *Literacy Without Frontiers*, edited by Freda Satow and Bill Gatherer, published by UKRA in 1992.

Material used in Chapters 5 and 6 was presented at the 29th UKRA Annual Conference at Exeter University in July 1992 and appeared in the conference proceedings, *Literacy: Text and Context*, edited by David Wray and published by UKRA in 1993.

CHAPTER 1

Readings

There are readings – of the same text – that are dutiful, readings that map and dissect, readings that hear the rustling of unheard sounds, that count grey little pronouns for pleasure or instruction and for a time do not hear golden or apples. There are personal readings, I am full of love, or disgust, or fear, I scan for love, or disgust, or fear. There are – believe it – impersonal readings – where the mind's eye sees the lines move onwards and the mind's ear hears them sing and sing.

Now and then there are readings which make the hairs on the neck, the non-existent pelt, stand on end and tremble, when every word burns and shines hard and clear and infinite and exact, like stones of fire, like points of stars in the dark – readings when the knowledge that we *shall know* the writing differently or better or satisfactorily, runs ahead of any capacity to say what we know, or how.

(A.S. Byatt, *Possession*, 1990)

When I read I escape into a dream world.
(From a Reading Autobiography by a twelve-year-old from North Tyneside. Collected by teacher Terry Brolly)

This book is about reading and readers. It is about what happens when readers engage with written texts – when the print is flashing in front of our eyes or the accompanying illustration catches our attention or a voice reads aloud to us, interpreting the words on the page. What is going on during these 'reading moments'? Are we just 'comprehending' the text, working out exactly what it 'means', and if so, how do we account for the different effects the same piece of writing has on different readers? Why does a particular story or poem move one reader to tears but leave another totally unmoved? Presumably, the same 'meaning' has been 'comprehended' by both readers as they both read the same words, so what has made the difference? As adults we recognize these reading differences, though we may never have given much thought to why they occur. We are also aware that we differ from each other in more fundamental ways. Some of us are avid readers for whom either novels or poetry or magazine stories or biographies (or all of them!) are a major part of our lives. We see ourselves as readers and not only need to immerse ourselves constantly in such works, but love sharing our enthusiasm with friends who are also readers. For others, reading means newspapers or factual books and magazines connected with a particular interest or with work. Fiction and poetry are never read (except perhaps for the once-a-year novel on the beach) and the attraction is something of a mystery. Why should this be? What lies behind the reading decisions we make as adults?

In the course of a day all of us read a great deal. Much of this reading happens without any conscious decision being taken by us to engage in it. The billboards move past our car windows as we drive to work as do the shop names and window displays. We follow road signs to 'London' or 'Manchester' without thinking about them. The scribbled shopping list or reminder on the kitchen calender are not thought of as reading. Only those who cannot read realize the power contained in all this 'environmental print'. For the great majority of adults, the same realization only occurs when we are faced with a totally alien script. Unless you can read Japanese, the example opposite will mean nothing. Because the symbols bear no resemblance to our alphabet, you cannot even 'say' the words (as you might be able to do in French or German).

Our 'automatic reading', then, happens all of the time and we take it for granted. It enables us to be a part of everyday life and to have some control over the lives we lead. We depend on it at home, in the street and at work. Later in this book, we examine one aspect, advertising, which forces its way into our lives whether we want it or not.

Some of us engage in reading beyond that needed to live and work. To use Frank Smith's (1988) term, we belong to a 'club' of like-minded people for whom reading is important beyond any utilitarian purpose. We love reading. We buy books and borrow them from libraries. We look forward to the times (hopefully every day) when we can sit back, pick up the book, open it, turn the pages and . . . read. We always have a book (or books) 'on the go', and as we find ourselves coming to the end of one we are already planning what the next will be. We have favourite authors and recognize that thrill of expectation when we hear their latest works have been published. We share our reading with friends who are also in the 'club', discussing what we have enjoyed recently, what has disappointed us and (just occasionally, but so importantly) the novel or story or poem which for some reason has impressed us and affected us so deeply that we add it to that list of works which we feel are 'great'. Despite the multitude of other attractions vying for our time, we still return to books.

6月になると、また ジマイマは、あ
たらしいたまごを うみました。そして、
それは だかせてもらいましたが、4つ
しか、ひなが かえりませんでした。

ジマイマは、ひなが ぜんぶ かえら
なかったのは、じぶんが しんけいしつに
なっていたからだと、いいました。でも、
ほんとうのことをいうと、ジマイマは
たまごをだく のが へたなのですよ。

If you are a 'reader' in the sense that you read at home novels, stories, poetry, you might pause for a few moments and wonder why. Just what is the attraction? Conversely, if you rarely make the conscious decision to read beyond the newspaper or something connected with your work, you might like to consider why not. Over the past five years, we have put such questions to hundreds of teachers and student teachers with whom we have worked. Within any group of twenty or thirty there will be some who are 'readers' and some who rarely read in their own time (even among groups of students taking literature courses!). The responses to the questions 'Why do you read?' and 'Why don't you read?' show a tremendous degree of agreement. The same answers turn up over and over again to the extent that we are able to predict confidently what the groups will be discussing and have previously prepared handouts to prove it. If we focus on story (magazine stories, short stories, novels), we always get words like 'pleasure', 'enjoyment', 'escape'. Everyone nods in agreement, but in fact these words can only be a starting point. What they mean in relation to reading is far from clear. After all, we both 'enjoy' eating in Indian restaurants, watching and playing sport and walking on the fells. All very different to reading a novel. What exactly do 'pleasure' and 'enjoyment' mean when applied to reading?

With regard to 'escape', reading seems even more complex. Just what are we escaping from or to? Perhaps there are clues in the following quotations:

> I become a thousand men and yet remain myself.
>
> (C.S. Lewis)

> Dwelling in possibility.
>
> (Emily Dickinson)

C.S. Lewis becomes involved in the lives of the characters of the novels he reads, so that at times he seems to be with them rather than in his own time and place reading about them. Emily Dickinson similarly recognizes in literature its power to involve her in the literary world. Perhaps it is to do with Tolkien's notion of the author creating a 'secondary world' into which the reader is invited (Tolkien 1964). The literary critic Wolfgang Iser describes reading in terms of the reader starting off 'outside' the text, well aware that he or she is in the real world and reading a book. Then something happens in the text and the involvement becomes so intense that for some seconds or even minutes the reader is in the text, unaware that he or she is really sitting in bed. Then the moment passes and the reader comes back out of the story world and is once more conscious of where he or she is and that he or she is simply reading a set of printed symbols on a page of paper:

> . . . we actually participate in the text, and this means that we are caught up in the very thing we are producing. That is why we often have the impression, as we read, that we are living another life.
>
> (Iser 1978)

Escape seems to be about the way readers can forget the worries and concerns of real life through involvement in the lives of the fictional characters in the stories they read. But whatever it means, readers seem to recognize it as vitally important and therefore we find ourselves wondering aloud whether work in the classroom is designed to foster such escape? If this is the big attraction for us as adults, surely it ought to be a major strategy in our attempts to develop a love of reading in children. Yet are we being unfair in suggesting that so often stories and novels, whether with infants, juniors, secondary pupils or university undergraduates, are approached in ways designed to prevent escape or involvement?

In the National Curriculum for English, we read in the programmes of study for Key Stage Two that children 'must learn to distance themselves from what they read'. In the reading Standard Attainment Task for Key Stage Three, powerful writing such as Christie Brown's *My Left Foot* is reduced to a comprehension passage with gaps to fill. The view expressed in the pamphlet *English, Whose English* produced by the Centre for Policy Studies (1987) that English literature is a body of knowledge which can be taught like any other body of knowledge, lies at the heart of a curriculum and forms of assessment which reduce the experience of reading to the level of the pub quiz. 'I know that Dickens wrote *David Copperfield* is all important; what it was like to read *David Copperfield* is irrelevant. Indeed, in the Key Stage Three anthology, children are not even reading *David Copperfield*. As Geoff Barton pointed out in the *Times Educational Supplement* (5 March 1993), the extract from the novel has been abridged: 'The dull bits, or the difficult bits, or the bits that don't quite fit, have been discretely dumped, the text re-worked as if intended for some junior version of Reader's Digest.'

Our work, which forms the basis of this book, suggests that what happens when we read is basically the same regardless of age. Indeed, the same process appears to be at work when very young children are read stories in the pre-school years. How they respond to *Goldilocks and the Three Bears* has much in common with how we respond to *Great Expectations*. Development from one to the other is due to our greater experience of life, of language and of different texts. Attempts to trace development in terms of psychological development have been made (e.g. Tucker 1981), but we would agree with Appleyard (1990) that such suggestions of a universal set of stages do not:

> . . . capture the gradual, incremental and multifaceted process by which development occurs in particular readers as they traverse a lifetime of stories, poetry and dramas. Nor can they take account of personal history, intelligence, personality traits, and unique likes and dislikes, which . . . may explain what is most distinctive about how a particular person reads. Neither can a schematic description of the main lines of development take more than a

partial account of factors such as gender, race, class and economic level by which the experience of large groups of readers is socially mediated.

We bring a great deal of ourselves to reading, whether we are very young or very old, so that reading is an intensely personal experience. In addition, we increase our 'literary competence' every time we read something which develops our understanding of what reading can be about and how texts can work. We take what we have learnt to whatever we read next. Much of this may well be unconscious learning, as we are too involved in what we are reading at the time to consider what we have learnt about 'literary technique'. Yet such learning is extremely important. In the early years, we see it when children re-tell stories they know or create their own stories, and in the next chapter this is illustrated with some fascinating examples. These children have not been taught formally how narrative works. They have learnt from the stories read to them. Their own stories contain features of the stories they have heard, such as a structure (beginning, middle and end) and consistent use of the past tense (what an amazing thing to have learnt!).

As adults we only become aware of our learning when faced with a text which does not seem to fit our ideas of how texts work. For example, when we first meet it, perhaps we are unsure what to make of the 'magical realism' of Gabriel Garcia Marquez. It may not be like anything else we have read. As a colleague commented, 'I've got nothing in my past reading to connect it to'. Indeed, the history of the arts can be seen in terms of artists extending the boundaries of what can be done. The shock to the literary establishment of *Lyrical Ballads* by Wordsworth and Coleridge in 1978 or the controversy surrounding the appearance of T.S. Eliot's *The Waste Land* in 1922 demonstrate vividly the process of coming to terms with new learning. The first exhibitions by both the impressionist and Pre-Raphaelite painters were greeted with great hostility by many art critics. All these examples are now so accepted and valued by us today that it is difficult for us to appreciate the passion and anger they once engendered. Similarly with a reader. The more and the wider we read, the more and wider we are able to read. As will be seen in Chapters 3 and 4, some of our adult readers were unable to come to terms with the opening of a particular novel we used with them. An opening such as that of Elizabeth Gaskell's (1854) *North and South* was not a problem. Everyone we worked with recognized it as a 'traditional' opening in which setting and characters are introduced. Some readers enjoyed it and wanted to read on; others indicated it had not interested them at all. But all readers knew where they were with it. They knew the rules which govern such openings, having read many like it. However, the opening page of Martin Amis's (1989) *London Fields* provoked very different reactions. A substantial number of readers confessed to being totally confused. They had no idea what what was going on, never having read an opening like this before. Some got quite angry, denouncing the first page (and the rest of the as yet unread novel!) vociferously. Others were equally confused but viewed this as something positive – a widening of their reading experience. The chapter on poetry shows similar issues being raised by the different poems we used to investigate the response of adult readers.

Just as the adults demonstrated the 'reading lessons' they had learned or were keen to learn (or had not learned and were definitely not keen to learn!) from their reading experiences, so children showed it was no different for them. Their responses to poetry in particular indicated the gulf already developing between those who knew and appreciated what poetry was about and those who did not and were unsure what a 'response' might look like. In the early years of schooling, we see the difference between children with rich experience of story and rhyme beginning to develop awareness of how these work and those for whom a story or a verse mean little. The ways in which the former use their awareness in the business of learning to read and write indicates how powerful are these early 'reading lessons'. Adults, ten-year-olds and four-year-olds, then, all engage in the same process. This must surely provide the basis for a rationale in terms of how we approach 'literature' (stories and poems) in the classroom.

We believe, therefore, that approaches to literature in the classroom should be based on the reading of it. If involvement and escape are key elements of the reading process, then let us explore what they mean. In so doing, we find ourselves drawn into texts and the ways they work as we demonstrate in later chapters. The areas providing the basis for work are, then, 'reading areas', and literature teaching springs from the powerful ways texts can affect us. The danger of ignoring reading in the desire to teach 'literature facts' faces us in the comments of teachers and students who do not read. So often their reasons show them looking back to experiences at school in which story and poetry were presented simply to be analysed. The switched-off reader of eight, eighteen or forty-eight sees no point in the exercise because, as Margaret Meek (1983) puts it:

> Readers are made when they discover the activity is 'worth it'. Poor, inadequate, inexperienced readers lack literary competence because they have too little idea of what is 'in' reading for them.

In order to become a reader, you first have to have an experience which affects you powerfully. Then you want it again. Before long you are hooked and cannot do without a regular fix·. For those of us who have developed the reading habit, learning more about the subject is fascinating: 'great' names from the past, techniques employed by writers, the new writer whose first novel creates a stir. All are part of belonging to the reading club. The aim of teaching must surely be to convince as many young readers as possible that this club is well worth joining. It will be a tragedy if another generation is put off reading by an over-emphasis, at too early an age, on analysis of extracts from some vague notions of literary heritage.

In the primary school, reading is often viewed from two different stand-points: 'the teaching of reading' and 'children's literature'. In the classroom, this might result in the child having different books, a 'reading book' and another book (what has become known as a 'real book'). There might be different lessons: some will focus on aspects of 'reading' with the child reading aloud to the teacher or attempting reading comprehension exercises; others will be opportunities to 'enjoy' books such as silent reading or teacher reading aloud to the class. Until fairly recently, this separation of reading from literature was also apparent at conferences and in books published on these areas. A 'reading conference' would be dominated by psychologists and linguists who used terms like digraphs, grapho-phonics, miscue analysis or initial teaching alphabet. A conference on children's literature would focus on the latest author-illustrators of picture books or the latest children's novelists, examining the dynamic between text and illustration or the ideology underlying particular works. Over the past few years, this division has begun to break down, though not without a certain amount of angst. At the 1992 conference of the United Kingdom Reading Association, the comment was made by one of the speakers that there was a 'problem' in that some of the speakers were from an 'English' background rather than a 'reading' background. The fact that this was seen as a 'problem' rather than a great opportunity showed how deep the division had been.

At its crudest, the division emerged with the move towards using 'real' books rather than reading schemes with young children learning to read; books which were written for 'escape' and 'involvement' rather than with the specific aim of helping a child read text correctly. Could children learn to read on children's literature or should learning to read and literature be kept apart? Certainly in many classrooms, children got the message: 'This is my reading book and this is not a reading book, just a book I enjoy'. Children sitting wide-eyed at the picture book *Not Now Bernard* or lifting the flaps and playing the game of *Where's Spot*, but learning to read on *Ginn 360* or *One, Two, Three and Away*. Whatever the arguments, according to HMI surveys, the vast majority of teachers are now making use of a variety of types of book, with those from schemes mixed with popular picture books. There is also growing awareness of how reading can be taught using texts of all sorts as contexts within which to examine the ways our writing system works. A story is easier to understand than the 'bits' which make it up. *Goldilocks and the Three Bears* is easier to understand than 'of' or 'b'. Starting with the story we can share its power with children and then use it to look at aspects of 'cracking the writing code'.

The realization that children are learning 'reading lessons' from their encounters with language in different contexts means that the worlds of reading theory and literary theory are becoming increasingly intermingled. One of the following quotations is taken from a book on 'reading', the other from a book about literary theory. Which do you think is which?

> Users cannot produce or decipher stories without some implicit competence in respect of narrative structure . . . This competence is acquired by extensive practice in reading and telling stories.

> Many of Chaucer's audiences must have been illiterate. Did they never appreciate the rhymes when they heard:
>
> 'Took her in his armes two and kiste her ofte,
> And her to glade he al his entente,
> For which her goost, that flickered all alofte,
> Into her woful herte again it wente'
> (Troilus and Criseyde)

In fact, the first is from *Narrative Fiction: Contemporary Poetics* by S. Rimmon-Kenan (1983) and is concerned with the development of literary competence. Although not a 'reading' book, it surely has implications for teachers in the early years. The second is from *Children's Reading Problems* by P. Bryant and L. Bradley (1985), in which research into the development of phonological awareness in children is linked to their experience of rhyme and alliteration, especially from nursery rhymes. While Chaucer in a book about reading problems might seem incongruous, the notion of powerful literacy contexts teaching valuable reading lessons is extremely important.

The next two quotations appear to be concerned with similar areas of reading, yet the intended audiences for the books from which they are taken are very different:

> Writing requries reading for its completion, but also teaches the kind of reading it requires.

> When I read with inexperienced readers I find that their difficulties lie not in the words but in understanding something that lies behind the words, embedded in the sense. It's usually an oblique reference to something the writer takes for granted that the reader will understand so that the text means more than it says.

Again the first is about literary theory, being from *The Modes of Modern Writing* by David Lodge (1977). It will be read by students at university studying literature at degree level. The second is from *How Texts Teach What Readers Learn* by Margaret Meek (1988), which is about reading with very young children. Yet both quotations draw our attention to fascinating aspects of children learning to read. In the next chapter, we examine Ruth Brown's

(1983) *A Dark, Dark Tale* as a text which 'teaches' three-year-old Dominic 'the kind of reading it requires'. Again, the ways in which reading and texts have so much in common regardless of the reader's age is exemplified.

Finally, a quotation from a book which might appear to be concerned with a different world to how readers respond to writing, *Specific Learning Difficulties (Dyslexia)*, by Peter Pumfrey and Rea Reason (1991):

> To summarise, the current view of 'schema' is of higher order, generic cognitive structures which underlie all aspects of human knowledge and skill. Although their processing lies beyond the direct reach of awareness, their products – words, images, feelings and actions – are central to involvement in literacy. These are the products children bring to the reading task which determine whether they become readers with a lifelong interest in books and other written information or whether they see reading as a job to be done through deciphering the text.

So, 'words, images, feelings and actions' are central to the business of learning to read and central to the lives of adult readers. This phrase draws attention to the basic notion of response which can be represented as:

READER ——————— INTERACTION ——————— TEXT

'Words' are what come out of texts and these words convey the author's intended meaning. But a great deal of the reader 'goes into' the text and interacts with it. It is this interaction between reader and text which is so fascinating and worth exploring, and 'images, feelings and actions' play a major part in it. Work in the classroom needs to recognize the nature of the interaction and be sensitive to the ways in which different readers respond to the same text. If each reader's reading is unique, then:

> [An interpreter's] object should . . . be not to explain a work, but to reveal the various conditions that bring about its possible effects . . . an interpreter can no longer claim to teach the reader the meaning of the text for without a subjective contribution and a context there is no such thing.
>
> (Iser 1978)

Challenging words indeed! What might the implications be on an undergraduate course? How might such a role for the teacher look in the early years? In fact, in each case the issue is the same and hinges on the need to explore the reader's part in the process as well as the text. Is it unfair to suggest that traditionally we have neglected the former and focused almost exclusively on the latter? So, in the early years we have asked questions about the stories we have read to children. At Key Stage Two, extracts from literature have been used as comprehension exercises designed to ascertain whether children have 'understood' a text. This process has continued into secondary classrooms, with the addition of searching for literary devices. During the past ten years or so, articles and books have appeared arguing for a methodology based on 'response' – for example, *Developing Response To Fiction* by Protherough (1983) and *Teaching Literature Nine to Fourteen* by Benton and Fox (1985). Indeed, in the original proposals for the English National Curriculum (June 1989), Michael Benton stated: 'The development of a methodology that is based upon informed concepts of reading and response rather than upon conventional, narrowly-conceived ideas of comprehension and criticism is now a priority.' Our work, then, follows the work of others and joins an ongoing debate about the best ways to approach literature in the classroom.

The National Curriculum English document incorporates response in the Attainment Targets but appears muddled with regard to primary school children. To achieve Level One, 'Speaking and Listening', children have to 'Listen attentively, and respond, to stories and poems'. But what will this look like? A faraway gaze at the teacher/reader's face? A smile, a laugh or a sigh? How will we know if it has happened and what sort of questions will allow us to assess it?

From Level Two, references to it are in the Reading Attainment Target and there is an attempt to define it in terms of both sides of the reading equation. To start with, though, Levels Two and Three do not really help much. Level Two is similar to 'Speaking and Listening', in that we have little idea of what is involved in response: 'Listen and respond to stories, poems and other materials read aloud, expressing opinions about what is being read'.

Level Three veers totally towards the text with references to setting, storyline, characters, significant detail, inference, deduction, meanings beyond the literal and 'some understanding of how stories are structured' (all to be attained by the average seven-year-old!). There is no indication of a personal response from the child.

Things begin to look up at Level Four: 'Describe those qualities of a poem or story which appeal and give an indication of personal response'. And at Level Five, we get the first clue as to what might be involved in this 'personal response': 'Discuss character, action, fact and opinion, relating them to personal experience'. Unfortunately, Level Six reverts to an agenda concerned solely with text, with mention of textual 'details' and 'reference to the text'.

It is interesting to note that Levels Seven to Ten (of relevance mainly to the secondary school) all refer explicitly to 'personal response'. Why not for each of the levels for younger children?

It is worth exploring further the references to 'response' in the English document, as they indicate the confusion which seems to lie at the heart of how to approach literature in the primary classroom. Teachers will search in vain for any guidance based on a clearly defined rationale. The word 'response' is defined in the Non-Statutory Guidance (para. 1.5):

Individual response to literature is fundamental to the programmes of study for reading. Readers respond to the same text in different ways at different times: readers make analogies between their own lives, current issues and those represented in texts, using the text as a fictional commentary on their own experience.

This is an excellent description of the process by which readers respond when reading and one would expect the programmes of study to reflect both the reader and the text in stipulating classroom work. However, in the programme of study for Key Stage Two ('response' is not mentioned in Key Stage One) we find:

Judgements about books will go beyond the mere expression of personal likes and dislikes. Children will start to distance themselves from what they read and reflect upon it, justifying reactions by reference to the text. They will begin to respond to books in terms of the ideas which they contain, as well as such things as character and plot.

Surely this was not written by the same person who wrote the definition of response? No mention now of the part played by the reader. All is focused on the text. Notice also the barely contained sneer in the use of 'merely' with regard to the development of personal taste in reading.

Not only, then, is guidance about how response might be explored in the classroom missing, but confusion about response runs through the document. It appears as if two different factions were at odds with each other and that the compromise was to include at least some references acceptable to each. The re-write, which appeared in June 1993, suggests that the arguments have been won, for there is an overwhelming approach exemplified (and what sad reading it makes). While this document may well end up on the dusty shelves of history, supplanted by the next sequel ('National Curriculum 3'!), we believe it is important to trace the ways response appears and to tease out the thinking that lies behind it. In the re-write, five pages describe the programmes of study and statements of attainment for reading but only the following mentions the part played by the reader:

The books and poems read and discussed should stimulate pupils' imagination and enthusiasm. They should include . . . interesting subject matter and setting which may be related to pupils' own experience or extend beyond their knowledge of the everyday.

The other six factors which should be included are all concerned with the text side of reading. We now have, though, an attainment strand called 'Response to Fiction', and might expect to find the above statement reflected in it. But no, only further references to texts and to children identifying likes and dislikes in their reading with no guidance as to what this might mean. The example provided for Level Three speaks volumes in terms of the status of personal response in these proposals: 'After reading "The Owl Who Was Afraid Of The Dark" by Jill Tomlinson, decide which character gives the baby owl, Plop, the best explanation for liking or enjoying the dark.' The fact that this lovely book casts such a spell on young children because of their own concerns about the dark, so that they identify with Plop, is not mentioned. That this would be worth exploring does not appear to count. Instead, we have to determine the advice of characters within the text, not the children who are reading it. How much more worthwhile to ask children what advice they might give Plop to help him to come to terms with his fears.

Key Stage Two of the re-write lacks even a single reference to the reader side of response and the power texts have to affect us deeply. Now pupils 'should be encouraged to respond imaginatively to the plot, characters, ideas and language in literature, to be able to refer to relevant passages or episodes to support their opinions', and 'They should be taught to consider some texts in more detail, e.g. by considering the actions of characters, the logic and consistency of the plot, and ideas conveyed, the writer's use of language'. The 'Response to Literature' strand reflects these textual concerns. We are not saying that how texts work should not be studied in primary school. Quite the opposite, and a great deal of this book explains how we believe texts might be approached. However, we do believe that ignoring the reader's response is a grave mistake and that examination of the text should proceed from a recognition of the ways it has affected us.

In fact, we never can 'measure' response. Indeed, we can never really even study it:

> We can never know exactly how an individual experiences . . . a story or a picture book.

> Observed response to literature is not equivalent to internal experience of literature.

(Crago 1985)

However, this does not mean that we cannot give status to the part played by the reader in the reading process. Indeed, we would argue that the reader is where the exploration of text ought to start. Trying to articulate what effect the text has had on different readers leads naturally into an examination of how the text brought about such an effect.

This work can begin in the early years and a good example is to focus on the 'pictures in the mind' readers produce when reading. These images owe something to both the text and the reader. We realize how personal they are if a film is made of a novel we have read and the hero or heroine does not look like we imagined. With five-year-olds we can read or tell a story aloud and ask the children to close their eyes and imagine the story. Discussion of what they 'see' can lead to an examination of the illustrations in the actual book and a comparison of them with the images produced by the children. The same basic idea can continue into the later primary years, secondary years and beyond. We have done it with groups of teachers. Working with older, more experienced readers leads them naturally back into the text to determine its contribution to the process. How the writer succeeds (or fails) in this respect involves looking at such areas as the use of language and literary devices. What the reader brings to reading leads, then, naturally to a consideration of how texts work.

However, while we certainly can consider 'how texts work', we can never tie down response. The danger of neglecting what the reader brings because it is not easily assessed (the trap into which the National Curriculum appears to have fallen – only teach what you can assess) leads to an arid view of reading in the classroom. As Arthur Koestler (1964) wrote: 'In order to love or hate something which exists only as a series of signs made with printer's ink, the reader must endow it with a phantom life, an emanation from his conscious or unconscious self.'

This chapter has been concerned with literature and the process which occurs as we read it. However, Chapter 5 examines response in a different area, that of advertising. As a result of our work with children and adults, we became interested in what response might look like in terms of different types of text. We chose advertising because it seemed to us that both sides of the process were clearly present. Advertisers certainly pay great attention to text, using many literary techniques in the writing. They are also aware of the part played by the reader and specifically target our views of ourselves and our dreams and desires in their work. Advertising plays a powerful role in our society and we wondered how 'literate' children were with regard to it. The study of advertising and its techniques has been a part of reading and English lessons for many years and in the National Curriculum it appears in the Programme of Study for reading at Key Stage Two: 'Teachers should discuss texts which make imaginative use of English – literature, advertising, songs, etc. – in order to bring out the ways in which the choice of words affect the impression given by the text.'

While it is not mentioned specifically in the attainment targets, references to 'media texts' are included in both Levels Five and Six. In preparing children for life in the twenty-first century, study of the ways in which advertising and other media work would seem to be essential. However, in the proposals for the re-write, all mention of advertising or 'media' has been removed. Quite why this should have happened we can only speculate upon. Why would it be thought unwise to have children study the ways these texts work? On television and in magazines they are certainly a major part of their lives.

Quite what the National Curriculum for Reading will eventually look like we will have to wait and see. Nevertheless, a close examination of what appears and what does not appear is vital if we are to be aware of the shifts of emphasis and the underlying views of those who determine the curriculum to be taught in primary schools. The proposals for the re-write, if accepted, would mean that a great deal of this book would become, officially, irrelevant to primary classroom teachers. No study of advertising and no status given to the part played by personal response in the reading of stories, novels, verse and poetry. An arid curriculum, with a watered-down version of literary criticism and the dry analysis of texts the only reading diet for young children. A National Curriculum for Reading which makes no mention of the ways texts affect readers is not much of a reading curriculum. No doubt there will be further attempts to re-write the English curriculum, but this does not devalue the above discussion. Whatever the 'final' document, there will be a need for an awareness of the view of reading which underlies it. Without such an awareness, we simply go through the motions in the classroom.

The anthology *Lifelines* (1993) is a collection of poems chosen by famous people, the brain child of a group of secondary pupils at Wesley College in Dublin. Attempting to explain why she chose Blake's 'Never Seek to Tell Thy Love', the novelist Margaret Drabble writes:

> I love this poem because it is sad – I have always liked sad poems best, I think – and because it is mysterious and yet compact and because it catches the difficulty and fragility of love. I don't really know what it means, but I respond to it very strongly.

The last sentence seems to be a contradiction in terms. How can she 'respond . . . very strongly' to something which she does not understand? Here is response and the ways in which it is always just out of the reader's grasp in terms of explaining it. Because so much of us is a part of how we respond to powerful writing, and this cannot be easily controlled, so our attempts at 'explaining its meaning' never match what we thought and felt while reading. In the same anthology, the novelist William Trevor writes:

> 'The Lady Of Shalott' is one of the poems I most enjoy, but to attempt to explain why that is would be like trying to explain why a certain food is a particular favourite. You cannot describe the taste of bananas or fresh peas. You cannot describe the magic of poetry.

A good job he is not trying to achieve Level Two of the National Curriculum re-write where he would have to join children having to 'Decide which of the stories . . . they prefer and explain why'. We wonder what 'reading lessons' children will learn from being asked to carry out such tasks.

The following chapters focus on readers (and in the next chapter children who have not yet learnt to read) and how they engage with different texts. Stories, novels, poems and advertisements have been used to examine what appears to be going on. While we never can get inside a reader's head to view the process exactly, we are convinced that discussion of the elements which contribute towards it should be the basis of work in classrooms.

CHAPTER 2

The power of story

And that night I took Grimm's Fairy Tales to bed and began to read, and suddenly the world of living and the world of reading became linked in a way I had not noticed before. 'Listen to this,' I said to Myrtle and Dots and Chicks. They listened while I read the Twelve Dancing Princesses, and as I read and they listened, I knew and they knew, gloriously, that *we* were the Dancing Princesses – not twelve but four; and as I read I saw in my mind the place in the neat cupboard in the corner of the bedroom where we could vanish to the underground world and the orchard that was 'our' orchard along the gully where the boughs of the trees honked and cried out when they were broken, silver and gold trees . . . And the shoes, danced each morning to shreds, we know about those, with our own shoe soles flapping from the uppers and Dad . . . complaining, like the king in the story. 'Where have you been that your toes are scuffed and your soles are worn through?' Where indeed!

(Janet Frame, *To the Is-Land*, 1982)

The above quotation from the New Zealand novelist Janet Frame's auto-biography captures beautifully the nature of the reader's response to litera-ture. The words always listed by teachers when asked why they, as adults, read ('escape', 'pleasure', 'involvement') were discussed in the last chapter and the meaning of those words shines through in Frame's description of her first encounter with Grimm's 'Fairy Tales'. The ways in which she and her sisters personalize the story of 'The Twelve Dancing Princesses', trans-forming the setting and the characters into their own lives, is a powerful aspect of the reading process for us all. We make connections between what we read, our lives and ourselves. As was stressed in the last chapter, we are not suggesting that the part played by the reader is all there is to the reading process. The ways texts work in determining how we read them is vitally important. However, traditionally, we have focused on the text in classrooms and used it as a comprehension exercise to extract its 'meaning'. We are arguing that such an approach only represents half of reading and that there is a need to redress the balance.

This chapter examines the interaction between the reader and the text in very young children and the same basic process will be seen to be at work as with the adults and older children discussed in other chapters. In all cases, there is both a reader side and a text side to the reading equation. This would seem to have implications for how we approach literature in the primary classroom, for work should surely be based on the ways in which we read. The danger is that we forget what really turned us into readers (or turned us off, as the case may be), so that we end up doing strange things to reading in the classroom. A gulf develops between the deeply felt responses we remember from our own childhood and which continue to take us to stories and poems as adults, and the work we give to the children we teach. In addition, we will be looking at what young children seem to be learning from their contact with stories and poems, much of it before they are able to read the texts for themselves. There are important implications here for the teaching of initial reading.

Responding to text: Dominic, aged three, shares *A Dark, Dark Tale* with his father

Ruth Brown's (1983) picture story book, *A Dark, Dark Tale*, is a beautiful example of the high-quality literature now available for young children. The text is supported by atmospheric illustrations and reads as follows:

> One upon a time there was a dark, dark moor.
> On the moor there was a dark, dark wood.
> In the wood there was a dark, dark house.
> At the front of the house there was a dark, dark door.
> Behind the door there was a dark, dark hall.
> In the hall there were some dark, dark stairs.
> Up the stairs there was a dark, dark passage.
> Across the passage there was a dark, dark curtain.
> Behind the curtain there was a dark, dark room.
> In the room there was a dark, dark cupboard.
> In the cupboard there was a dark, dark corner.
> In the corner there was a dark, dark box.
> And in the box there was . . . A MOUSE!

Three-year-old Dominic was videotaped sharing this book with his father and the result enables us to glean something of the ways in which this young child responds to a book which is obviously a favourite. The two of them are seen sitting comfortably, cuddled up to each other, with the book open on Dominic's lap. In the course of fifteen minutes or so, they go through the book three times, Dominic insisting on beginning again each time they finish. This is despite his father's best efforts to introduce a new book *(Thomas the Tank Engine)!* Each of the three readings contains different elements and together they appear to progress from a straight rendition of the text in the first to commenting on the text and illustrations in the second to Dominic introducing a number of fascinating new dimensions to his response in the third. Throughout all three, he stares intently at the illustrations, often for some moments so that his father feels obliged to make a comment or provide a prompt to get things moving again. Of course, we will never know exactly what is going on in his mind during these moments of intense deliberation, but the fact that he eventually does begin to verbalize his thoughts seems to indicate a settling both with the book and the situation. Perhaps he felt a need to demonstrate his competence initially: to show his father that he knew the book. His father does comment between the second and third readings that 'mummy' has told him how well Dominic could 'read' the books.

The first reading is, then, Dominic reciting the text almost word perfectly (given one or two hints from his father). He does not stop to comment on the text or give any indication as to how he might be responding to it. His enjoyment is simply conveyed by the intonation he uses to convey the text. He cannot yet read and his ability to do this is obviously based on the book having been read to him on many previous occasions. Now the illustrations provide the cues for the text. The fact that he can achieve an almost perfect reading from memory is due as much to the quality of the text as to his own ability.

In Chapter 1, we quoted the literary critic David Lodge (1977): 'Writing requires reading for its completion but also teaches the kind of reading it requires'. Ruth Brown's text certainly 'teaches the kind of reading it requires' and Dominic is able to provide the necessary dramatic intonation right through to the sudden cry of 'A mouse!' and his father's reaction of 'surprise'. The text achieves this because it is such a cohesive text. The basic sentence structure and many of the words are repeated on each page so that each stage in the narrative coheres closely to the previous stages. It is highly patterned at the level of words, sentence structures and text structure. As John Stephens (1992) states:

> Such cohesive repetition is, of course, also desirable in narratives for young audiences who have not yet developed a strong sense of connectedness in narrative. Clearly, a series of utterances which are linked by strong cohesion but which also contain new actions build on whatever grasp of narrativity an audience may have, and may even help to foster a developing sense of narrative, of relatedness of utterances and events, and of cause-and-effect relationships.

To produce a powerfully dramatic text with these features is not easy (as any children's writer knows!). It is the reason for the appeal of traditional fairy tales, many of which contain almost ritual, repetitive sections – 'Who's been sleeping in my bed?' . . . – with which children can join in.

The second 'reading' begins immediately:

Dominic:	And on the dark, dark moor there was a dark, dark wood.
	In the dark wood there was a dark, dark, house.
	Behind the dark, dark house there was a dark, dark door.
	[mumbles]
	In the . . .
Father:	Behind the door.
D:	There was a big – dark, dark . . .
	Oh there's a pussy cat running up the steps!
	There's no-one in that house.
F:	No-one in the house is there not?
D:	No.
F:	What's on the next page?
D:	In . . . in . . . in . . .
F:	In the hall.
D:	There was a dark, dark stairs . . .
[F:	. . . stairs]
D:	And up the stairs there was a dark, dark passage.
[F:	Oh!]
D:	And up the passage there was a dark, dark . . . and then –
F:	There was a dark, dark . . . what? C-
D:	Curtain.
F:	Curtain.
D:	Look! There's a pussy going in!
F:	Pussy cat going in.
D:	In the dark, dark curtain there was a dark, dark room . . .
	I don't know.
F:	That's a rocking horse isn't it?
D:	Yes.
F:	[whispers] What's on the next page. Let's see.
D:	There's – there's a curtain.
	In the – look there's a pussy cat!
F:	Yes – in the dark – in the room there was a . . .
D:	Look! There's no-one in there.
F:	[exasperated!] Yes – but what is it? It's a dark, dark . . .?
D:	That's a pussy cat. It's cross.
F:	It's cross?

D: [whispers] Yes. In the room there was a dark, dark cupboard.
       And in the cupboard there was a c- . . . all the things . . .

F: It's in a dark, dark corner wasn't it?

D: No, that's not a dark, dark corner.
       That's a dark, dark cupboard.

F: Oh, that's a . . .

D: That's all the toys! No-one's playing with them.

F: No-one plays with them? Why's that?

D: That . . . that . . . that's all the children's toys – and the chil-
       dren have left them there.

F: They've left them there?

D: Yes.

F: They've left them tidy haven't they.

D: Yes.

F: Not like yours!

D: Look!

F: In the corner was a . . .

D: Dark, dark box. In the box there was a – in the box – in the
       cupboard there was a dark, dark box – and in the box there was
       a MOUSE!!

F: Oh! My God! What a fright!

The second reading finishes as the first had done with Dominic grinning as he shouts 'mouse' and his father registering the appropriate reaction.

What always seems to be a feature of conversations between pre-school children and adults is the children being very much in charge and the adult leading from behind. This is no exception. Dominic has his own agenda and is determined to speculate on the story. His father wants to stick to the text (after all he has been through it once already!) but is not always successful in hurrying up the reading. Teachers know the pressures in the classroom which can so often lead to shared reading (or just listening to a child read) being simply a child getting through text with scarcely time to draw breath. Yet without such time we risk giving children (and ourselves?) a narrow, restricted view of reading. Faced with Dominic's comments and the long, silent pauses where he gazes at the pictures, the need to provide time for response seems so important.

Dominic focuses on the cat which appears in each of the illustrations and then on the toys scattered in the room. Texts tell one story, but in the best picture books the illustrations do not simply reflect the text. Rather they extend it, offering possibilities and opportunities for the reader to create their own scenarios. We fill in the 'gaps' left by writers and illustrators with our own speculations and connections. Maurice Sendak has explained his decision not to draw Max's mother in his classic *Where the Wild*

Things Are (1967), as he wanted each child reader to fill this gap with their own mothers. The adult readers in Chapters 2, 3 and 4 are shown engaged in exactly the same process. No matter how much a writer tries to make something explicit, there will be gaps in the writing which readers fill. So, in Dominic's reading, the cat is 'cross' (though he does not tell us why) and a pile of toys leads to speculation about the children who 'have left them there'. In fact, the whole of Ruth Brown's text is one enormous gap as we are never told anything about the house (Who lives there? Why is it empty?). Each reader has to ask the same questions but there are no correct answers. This really is a text we have to interrogate. Indeed, perhaps there never are right answers in literature, as each reader brings his or her own agenda to the reading. There may be common ground between readers at a superficial level but (as Iser points out) we do not find ourselves drawn to literature for meaning. Rather, it is the 'significance' of the text for each reader which really matters and right and wrong answers do not apply at that level.

In this second reading, then, Dominic comments on the illustrations and the stories outside the text at which they are hinting. Now his father is determined to introduce *Thomas the Tank Engine*, but Dominic will have none of it. First he plays with *A Dark, Dark Tale*, holding it under the light while chanting 'Now it's light', and then on his lap. 'And now it's dark'. He repeats this over and over again as if the physical light and darkness reflect the darkness in the tale. When handed *Thomas the Tank Engine*, he grips it tightly and announces dramatically, 'No, it won't open. It won't open'. Finally, his father admits defeat and the third reading beings:

Dominic: No, I'm going to read this again.
  Once upon a . . . there was a dark, dark moor.
Father: Mmmm.
D: And in the dark, dark moor there was a dark, dark house.
  Look! There's no-one in!
F: No it wasn't. It was a dark, dark wood first.
D: Dark, dark wood first.
F: Turn the page. Go on.
D: In the dark, dark wood there was a dark, dark HOUSE!
F: Oh!
D: And behind there was a dark, dark door.
  Look there's a pussy cat. Who's that pussy cat?
F: I don't know. Who is it?
D: I know of that. It's a pussy cat who lives next door.
F: Oh it lives next door does it?
D: Yes.
F: Oh.

D:	Lives next door . . . Look no-one lives there. No-one lives there. No-one lives there any more.
F:	Why is that?
D:	Because it's dark!
F:	It's dark. Oh.
D:	Yes . . . That's a church.
F:	Looks like a church does it?
D:	Yes. It is a church.
F:	Do you think so?
D:	Yes, it is a church. I told you. That's a church.
F:	Oh, I thought that was a dark, dark hall.
D:	That's not a dark, dark hall. That's a church.
F:	Oh. Has the pussy cat gone to church?
D:	No, it's gone to next door.
F:	Oh, it's gone next door.
D:	Yes. People stroked pussy cat. You had horses when you were old . . . young . . . when you were a boy of three.
F:	When you were?
D:	Grandma runs after you when you were a little boy.
F:	Grandma runs after you when you were a little boy? Why's that?
D:	Yes because . . . look! In . . . in the corner.
F:	No. In the hall.
D:	In the . . . in the church there was a dark, dark stairs. Up and down dark stairs there was a dark, dark, passage.
F:	Oh . . .
D:	[whispers] And in the curtain – up – there was a big curtain.
F:	What was behind the big curtain?
D:	Look! Pussy cat!
F:	I thought the pussy cat had gone next door.
D:	No, it went upstairs.
F:	It went upstairs did it?
D:	Yes. And – went behind the curtain.
F:	Did it?
D:	Yes.
F:	And what's behind the curtain? [Dominic slams the book shut]
F:	What have you done that for?
D:	I didn't want to read it.
F:	Oh! That's very good isn't it. Are you going to read Thomas?
D:	Mummy stop holding the camera. I'm going to read a story to daddy.

The third and final reading, then, never reaches the dramatic discovery of the mouse. Dominic appears to have had enough of the story! However, we see a number of fascinating aspects of response in the dialogue with his father. First, as in the previous reading, he speculates beyond the actual tale being told. The fact that there are no people to be seen leads to 'Look, there's no-one in' and 'Look, no-one lives there. No-one lives there. No-one lives there. No-one lives there any more'. In addition, the cat has gone 'next door'. This filling of gaps has been discussed above and these further examples illustrate again the importance of this process in reading. Second, he imposes his own interpretation on the illustrations despite his knowledge of the text. The hall is pictured with a stained glass window which leads Dominic to assert (despite his father's suggestion to the contrary) that it is in fact a church: 'Yes, it is a church. I told you. That's a church'. He holds on to this idea throughout the subsequent discussion so that when his father eventually draws him back to the text with 'In the hall', he re-asserts 'In the . . . [pause for thought] . . . church . . .'. What are we to make of this? Certainly, in a strict sense, he is wrong, and were he older and being tested on this book he would not be awarded any marks for suggesting that the picture showed a church. But when faced by a story or a poem which is particularly powerful, do not all readers find themselves personalizing it? We are reminded of something important in our own lives and so we read it into the text. The epigraph at the beginning of Chapter 1 from A.S. Byatt's (1990) *Possession* recognizes that sometimes, 'There are personal readings, that snatch for personal meanings. I am full of love, or disgust, or fear, I scan for love, or disgust, or fear'.

As was suggested above, we gain meaning from a text at the 'surface level' – meaning on which there would be general agreement – but below the surface the text will have a different 'significance' for each reader. The power of a work of literature lies in significance and to focus solely on surface meaning is to reduce the experience to an arid exercise.

In her autobiography (quoted at the beginning of this chapter), Janet Frame (1982) describes the death of her older sister, Myrtle, in a drowning accident. Not long afterwards she is given a poetry book at school: 'I began to explore the poetry book, and to my amazement I discovered that many of the poets knew about Myrtle's death and how strange it was without her'. This lovely statement captures the power of the process whereby we make particular works of literature 'our own'. It also makes us realize how much of the power of literature is lost when we become concerned only with matters of correctness, of getting the right answer to someone else's question. How important it is for Dominic to insist that the stained glass hall is, for him, a church.

The third feature of Dominic's final reading is, perhaps, the most interesting of all, and again points to something that all readers do. While discussing the cat, Dominic suddenly, and for no apparent reason, veers off onto something completely different:

Dominic: Yes. People stroked pussy cat.
You had horses when you were old . . . young . . . when you were a boy of three.
Father: When you were?
D: Grandma runs after you when you were a little boy.

Something in the text or the illustrations has triggered these thoughts. Like his insistence that the hall is a church, Dominic is personalizing the book, but unlike that example his comments now do not appear to have anything to do with the book at all. In the next two chapters, we see adults doing exactly the same thing, only they are able to indicate the word or phrase which is the trigger. We call this 'free-wheeling' and examine the difference between the 'denotative' meanings of words (the basic meanings we all share) and 'connotative' meanings (which are personal). For example, we all share a basic, common understanding of the word 'home' (denotative – the meaning of the word), but each one of us has different thoughts and feelings when we come across it in our reading due to our different experience of what 'home' means (connotative – the significance of the word for each of us). Once again we are faced with a major feature of what it means to experience literature, which is very difficult to quantify in terms of right and wrong answers to questions about the 'meaning' of texts. If, in order to test literature, we focus only on the denotative meanings, we again reduce the experience and ignore something which we all appear to do. In this context, we need to ask whether Dominic's comments above are of no relevance or value and best ignored or whether they are to be encouraged as part of the richness of response? And what of a nine-year-old discussing a poem or story? Or a sixteen-year-old? Or a twenty-five-year-old?

We have focused in detail on one example of a young child responding to a picture story book in order to demonstrate the richness of that response. Parents and teachers of young children will recognize the different elements but also be aware of the difficulty of allowing time for the process to weave its magic. The harassed parent who declared that the best bedtime story books were the shortest speaks for most of us at some time in our children's lives! Dominic's father certainly allows his son time to engage with the text, but also tries to impose his pace on the proceedings. How many infant teachers have held up a book which shows a kitten on the cover to be greeted with choruses of 'I've got a kitten like that'/'My kitten died last week'/'My dad is selling our kittens'/'Our cat is going to have kittens'. The often heard 'How interesting but we must get on with the story' is understandable in the busy infant classroom, but also presents a challenge in terms of developing strategies which will allow children the time to respond and which demonstrate that we value what they bring to the stories and poems we share with them. If we believe that personal response is the way into a love of books and reading, we surely have to find time for it in the classroom.

The two 'sides' of the reading process – what the reader brings and what the text brings – both play important roles in Dominic's response to *A Dark, Dark Tale*. In terms of the latter, Ruth Brown has written and illustrated a text which not only has tremendous power for a child, but which uses repetition at both word and sentence level to build to the climax. It is a text which Dominic can recite because he has internalized the basic sentence structure and the text structure. He has a clear 'map' in his mind of where each sentence is going and where the text as a whole is going. One can see how recognition of some of the words will be a natural outcome of repeated sharing, especially if the adult draws attention to them by running a finger along the text as it is being told and perhaps looking back at some of them after the story has finished ('That's the word "dark". Can we find it on another page?'). The words emerge from the text and sentence structures, which in turn have only been internalized because the book is such a powerful experience. The ways in which experience of written texts results in children becoming aware of, and sensitive to, different aspects of written language is fundamentally important in considering approaches to the teaching of initial reading. We realize how much more there is to learning to read than either word recognition or letter–sound correspondences. Both of these are, of course, a vital part of reading, but the continued references to them in the media as if they were all that were involved simply demonstrates the ignorance of so-called 'education correspondents'. Yet our experience suggests that there are still some early years teachers who see the teaching of reading as polarized between 'whole-word' and 'phonic' approaches. The advocation of 'mixed methods' means, then, simply using both 'whole-word' and 'phonic' approaches in the classroom. In so doing, the learning we are considering in this chapter is ignored. It is interesting to read the latest re-write of the Reading Attainment Target and see what messages are implied in it.

Dominic's ability to tell the story while he turns the pages demonstrates what he has so far learned about reading. Another way of finding out what non-readers can do (before assuming that because they cannot yet decode they know nothing about reading) is for them to re-tell favourite stories and rhymes from memory. Four-year-old Kyle, at nursery school, was asked to do just this and chose the traditional tale of 'The Three Little Pigs'.

Once upon a time there was three little pigs.
And mummy pig said, "You are nearly grown to your own size and must go in the woods and do your own house".

And then they went off and she reminded them . . . then . . . eh . . . then . . . do you know what happened? She said . . . she 'minded them of the wolf. And off they went and they said they'll be careful. So off they went . . . eh . . .

No. The little . . . the other wolf . . . the other little . . . the other piggie went to build a straw. And this man came along with some straw and the little piggie said, "May I have some of your straw, men, to build a house?"

And she said, "Yes, why for? You're a polite little pig".

And then the little wolf came along and he said, "LITTLE PIG, LITTLE PIG, LET ME COME IN!"

And he said, "NO, NO, NO. NOT BY THE HAIR OF MY CHINNY CHIN CHIN!"

So he said, "THEN I'LL HUFF AND I'LL PUFF AND I'LL BLOW YOUR HOUSE DOWN!"

And then he huffed and he puffed and he huffed and he puffed and he blew the little piggie's house down together again.

Then the other little pig was getting some wood . . . and the other little pig was getting some wood . . . and he found – this man came along and he said . . . and the little pig said, "May I have some of your sticks to build a house?"

And he said, "Yes, you're a polite little pig".

And he builded it.

And then the big, bad wolf came along and he said, "LITTLE PIG, LITTLE PIG, LET ME COME IN!"

And the little pig said, "NO, NO, NO, NOT BY THE HAIR OF MY CHINNY CHIN CHIN!"

And he said, "THEN I'LL HUFF AND I'LL PUFF AND I'LL BLOW YOUR HOUSE DOWN!"

So he huffed and he puffed and he huffed and he puffed and he blew the little piggie's house down and he ran into the woods, escaping.

And then the other little pig was more polite[?] from his little brothers and he thought, "It's got to be hard. I'm going to have to build some brick ones".

And then . . . and he taked a long time and some of his friends who lived in the woods . . . he decided they could help him . . . and then they builded it . . . and then he invited all his friends into his new house . . . and then he did a beautiful dinner for them they ever seed.

And then the little, bad wolf – the big, bad wolf came along and he said, "LITTLE PIGGIE, LITTLE PIGGIE LET ME COME IN!"

And he said, "NO, NO, NO, NOT BY THE HAIR OF MY CHINNY CHIN CHIN!"

And he said, "THEN I'LL HUFF AND I'LL PUFF AND I'LL BLOW YOUR HOUSE DOWN!"

And he said, "Oh no you won't!"

So he huffed and he puffed and he huffed and he puffed and he huffed and he puffed and he huffed and he puffed and he couldn't blow the little piggie's house down.

Then . . . No – he just does it on the book not doesn't it on the story.

And then he decided to go down the chimney . . . and they could hear . . . so they jumped outside and he decided a big water . . . hot boiling water . . . and then they did it in the fireplace and they went in and he went SPLASH in it. And then they didn't see it . . . and it didn't cause any trouble all the time . . . and then they lived happily ever after.

Kyle's telling of this story is tremendously dramatic, his intonation and changes in volume impossible to transcribe. The almost ritualistic parts are indicated in capital letters but one cannot capture the way he elongates 'blow' with a rise and fall of his voice so that it lasts some seconds. Listening to it we are aware of what an achievement it is for such a young child. In addition, Kyle is very much telling *his* story, so that when a girl brings over a picture book of 'The Three Little Pigs' and tries to suggest what might happen next, Kyle insists, 'No, he just does it on the book not doesn't it on the story'. The text is there to be personalized just as Janet Frame personalizes the *Twelve Dancing Princesses* and Dominic parts of *A Dark, Dark Tale*. The power of a text lies in what it means to a particular reader. As with Dominic, however, the quality of the text plays an absolutely vital role. Kyle has learned how this text needs to be 'read', with the repetition of incident and build up to the climax providing the scaffold. The use of rhyme ('he huffed and he puffed') and alliteration ('chinny chin chin') are also props and will be developing his sensitivity to the sounds in words. Such phonological awareness has been shown to be an extremely important predictor of the ease with which children learn to read, gained also from nursery and other rhymes (Goswami and Bryant 1991).

An important aspect of the part played by the text in response is the way in which readers develop literary competence through their encounters with different texts. Each text provides further evidence of the possible ways in which texts work, so that we learn from what we read and take that learning to the next text. In the next chapter, some adult readers are shown struggling with the opening of a Martin Amis novel, not because they cannot understand the words but because they have not encountered a novel which is written in that particular way. A similar problem can be encountered with children at Key Stage Two when faced with the works of writers like Alan Garner or Philippa Pearce and has major implications for how we approach reading in junior classes. This aspect of Kyle's literary competence means that he will take important awareness to the business of learning to read. Awareness of how story works and the sorts of language involved. He will no doubt have expectations of reading. As teachers, we need to be aware of what he *can* do (even though he cannot yet read a word), his expectations and how we might build on what he has already learnt, using it in our teaching approaches.

What young children learn from sharing books and stories in the pre-school years can also be gleaned by moving on a stage from Kyle's re-telling of a favourite story to children composing their own stories. Thomas (aged four years nine months) is the son of a colleague of ours, Kath Langley. In the bath one night he told the following story which he called 'Loads of Elves and One Wizard and Some Hobbits':

> Once upon a time there was some elves and some hobbits . . . and they asked Bilbo the hobbit to come on a long journey with them to find some treasure . . . and off they went for the journey to begin . . . and they all met at a nice stream . . . and they saw a boat on this stream with a flag – a orange flag . . . and it seemed to be sailing to them and when it got very, very close they saw that it had something that they didn't like – vultures . . . they were very bad to them – the vultures . . . and the boat hit the earth and the flag fell off and they rowed around looking for their flag and it wouldn't stay still for them . . . and they put it back on . . . then they landed and I'll tell you about it . . . no-one could see them – the vultures except Bilbo . . . he turned himself invisible and he wacked the vultures and the vultures flew away and landed in the water . . . the tide was going too quickly and the boat sinked – sank . . . the earth shivered and the mountain fell on top of the boat and broke the vultures and the boat . . . vultures are bad so it's alright if they're dead and get hurt . . . Suddenly Gandalf said a magic word and it shivered the earth and . . . and he put a spell and it put the mountain up and the elves got across the water and got the sea horses and the crabs and the octopuses to help them with their journey . . . when they met a bad monster the octopus jumped up and the monster melted in the river because he was made out of ice cream . . . he just melted away.

In the stories children compose themselves, we see what they have learnt as a result of having stories read and told to them. This learning is just the beginning of a process which continues in readers throughout their lives, so that again we are struck by the commonality of what is going on when very young children encounter story and what happens when adults read novels. It can be viewed as two different elements, the first of which is summarized by Gordon Wells (1986):

> Through listening to stories, children . . . extend the range of their experience far beyond the limits of their immediate surroundings. In the process they develop a much richer mental model of the world and a vocabulary with which to talk about it.

This statement comes towards the end of a book in which research in Bristol into factors in the pre-school years which might determine success with learning at school is described. The major factor isolated by the research (and it is a fascinating piece of work) is the learning which results from children sharing books and stories in the home. This is the single biggest predictor of later success at school. However, the quotation could equally apply to adults reading novels, and we are reminded of the quotations in the last chapter concerning what happens when we read:

I become a thousand men and yet remain myself.

(C.S. Lewis)

Dwelling in possibility.

(Emily Dickinson)

The same process and the same learning, then, from a toddler listening to a fairy tale to an adult reading Dickens.

'Loads of Elves and One Wizard and Some Hobbits' certainly demonstrates this learning. Kath's son Thomas is obviously 'dwelling in possibility', and in the words of Gordon Wells has definitely gone 'far beyond the limits of . . . [his] . . . immediate surroundings'! The vocabulary speaks for itself and clearly has come from contact with the world of books and stories. While Thomas has not yet read *The Hobbit* nor had it 'officially' read to him, he has older brothers from whom he has learned about this fantasy world. This leads to the second element in the learning, which is of more direct relevance to this book: what readers learn about reading from stories and novels. In the last chapter, we outlined the two sides of the reading process – the reader and the text – and discussed how we learn about the text through reading, developing 'literary competence'. We take our learning of how texts can work to each new text. In the next chapter, we see this happening in adults and older children, but the beginnings can be seen in Thomas's story. All of the stories he has heard so far have enabled him to learn important lessons about the world of stories and how they work.

First, there is the drama and the power: 'Suddenly Gandalf said a magic word and it shivered the earth and . . . and he put a spell and it put the mountain up and the elves got across . . .'. The power is what draws children into stories and anyone who has ever read aloud to them knows that this is so. At the really exciting bits, their eyes are fixed intently on us and yet have a glazed faraway look in them. They are holding their breath, mouths open, and there is an intensity in the room which is difficult to describe. This does not occur at any other time in the school day and every time it happens we find ourselves wondering at the power of story to so affect children (the same power, of course, which holds an adult reader). This is one of the great motivators for children learning to read. They will be able to read for themselves the stories others are reading to them.

Second, there are the aspects of written text which Thomas demonstrates he has learned from the stories read to him. So the story is structured, beginning with the conventional opening, introducing the characters, describing their adventures and coming to a resolution in which good triumphs over evil. This is the way so many stories go and Thomas has internalized the pattern. He will therefore have expectations of new stories, assuming that they will fit this pattern. Again adults can form similar expectations and be thrown by a story (or novel) which deviates from them (as we see in the next chapter). Then there is the consistent use of the past tense. Pronouns are used to eliminate repetition and to act as cohesive ties which hold the text together. There is an impressive mixture of simple, compound and complex sentences. Not bad for four years nine months! In fact, the learning about written language and narrative text which Thomas demonstrates in his story is tremendously impressive. Children like him have learnt so much from their contact with stories and they will use this learning in the task of becoming literate. As they learn to read, they need to encounter texts with different structures or which use language in different ways so they will take this increasing literary competence to the next text. While children certainly do need to be able to 'decode' the words on the page, we see how much more there is to reading than that. Similarly, they make use of their learning when they write. Indeed, Thomas's story is very much his own written composition (just as if we dictate a letter to a secretary it is our letter) and we see how much more there is to becoming a writer than handwriting and spelling. In a very real sense, children learn to write by reading (and by listening to others read aloud to them), unconsciously internalizing the forms and structures of writing so that they know how writing works. On 'Desert Island Discs', Norman Tebbit described his growing awareness as a child of his ability to write. He then discussed how important this ability had been for him as a young man. Interviewing him, Sue Lawley asked whether he had been a reader and Tebbit responded very positively with memories of being read to and then his own reading. However, neither of them then made the connections between the reading and the writing. Yet how often are we told by politicians or media correspondents that skills training and explicit grammar teaching are the key to writing. The stories young children tell us before they can write for themselves demonstrate where the secret really lies.

Out of powerful contexts, then, children learn reading and writing lessons which are vital for the development of literacy. The experience of reading implicitly teaches a child what reading and writing are all about. Of course, there are other lessons which have to be learnt and which teachers will have to make explicit, centring on the ways in which our alphabetic system works – how written symbols represent sounds.

But making such knowledge about language explicit, standing back from the functions and forms of writing (of which stories and poems are but two), and focusing on the ways language and print 'work', makes so much more sense if the writing is embedded in a context which makes sense to the child. As was mentioned in Chapter 1 for young children who have had access to a rich diet of stories, 'Goldilocks and the Three Bears' will be easier to understand than 'b'. The word 'bear' and then, perhaps, the letter 'b', can however be examined, recognized and understood as part of this favourite text. Words and letters can then be taken to other texts. The important point is that we recognize the learning children do about reading which precedes an explicit focus on our writing system. This learning is about the power of stories and poems and the ways they reflect ourselves and our lives – what readers take to texts and what they get from texts; learning about the ways texts work and the 'rules' which apply to them – the literary competence readers develop. These are the two sides of the reading process: the reader and the text.

The focus in this chapter has been on literature, but the same points could be made about the other powerful texts children will encounter and wonder at: Christmas cards, television adverts, packaging, labels, etc. As texts, each will teach reading lessons because each one works in a different way, so adding to a reader's repertoire in terms of knowing how written language can be constructed and used. As readers, children will bring knowledge and awareness based on previous encounters with these texts or of what they are about. This environmental print can then be used in classrooms as a way into learning about the writing system. A kicking 'k' as the first letter of Kelloggs begins to make connections for children between reading and life, providing another context for the development of literacy.

This chapter has been concerned with pre-school children who cannot yet read. Yet the ways in which they respond to literature and begin to develop literary competence connects them directly with the older children and adults discussed in the following chapters. The same processes are seen to be at work whether we are examining a three-year-old listening to a story or an adult reading a novel. In both cases, listeners/readers bring a great deal of themselves to the text, making connections both with themselves and the texts they have already encountered. In both cases, texts make demands on listeners/readers and we build up literary competence which enables us to meet those demands. For parents at home and early years teachers in the classroom, examples of transcripts and dictated stories such as we have collected demonstrate the importance of reading aloud to children and sharing books with them. We do not read aloud to children just because it is 'nice' or relaxing or a treat at the end of the day (when the basics have been worked at all morning), but because reading aloud teaches children so much about literacy. Nothing could be more basic than the reading lessons children learn at these times.

As children begin to crack the code, so they become part of the world of readers. They join Frank Smith's Literacy Club. Now they can read, the challenge is to keep them reading so that they grow into adults for whom reading is important beyond the utilitarian needs of everyday life. Ahead of them lies the world of novels and poetry which offers so much in terms of powerful reading experiences. To gain the most from it, they must further develop their literary competence. It is to the ways readers read and respond to such texts and the demands the texts make on readers that we now turn.

CHAPTER 3

Readers and stories

One thing is immediately clear to you: namely that this book has nothing in common with the one you had begun.

(Italo Calvino, *If on a Winter's Night a Traveller*, 1979)

That is what reading is: rewriting the text of the work within the text of our lives.

(Roland Barthes, 'Day by day with Roland Barthes', 1985)

A good teacher should be sceptical of originality in response to literature because it is most likely to betray a failure of understanding. The competent reader reads a work of literature much as other competent readers read.

(John Marenbon, Chair of SEAC)

One of the fascinating features of Dominic's reading of *A Dark, Dark Tale* is that he has no inhibitions about stepping right outside the text and interpreting it in the light of his own experience of the real world. Despite, or perhaps because of, the fact that he does not yet know the rules involved in responding to a text, he had no qualms about providing his own gloss on it. Can this, in John Marenbon's words, be regarded as a 'failure of understanding'? Or does Dominic's way of approaching *A Dark, Dark Tale* provide us with an important insight into how readers approach text in the early years but lose as they move into classrooms where there is little to encourage and stimulate such individual readings?

In this chapter, we continue to explore the nature of response within the context of adults and older primary children. What happens when 'real' readers engage with narrative? How far are the responses of such readers different from and similar to Dominic's? What can such responses tell us about our task as teachers of reading? If we accept John Marenbon's point quoted above, this task seems to be a straightforward one of teaching word recognition and the 'appropriate' response to a particular book. We feel this to be a depressingly narrow view of what reading is all about. Moreover, it helps to explain why thousands of sixteen-year-olds never want to read novels again after enduring traditional examination courses in English literature.

In addition to exploring the nature of response in readers, we also want to investigate the types of demand that narrative texts make on readers. By focusing on key elements of the reader's response on the one side and demands of the text on the other, we hope to highlight features which will have important implications for the primary classroom. Obviously, we want teachers to encourage the type of individual response hinted at in the Roland Barthes quote at the head of the chapter, yet we also need to channel individual responses to try to ensure that pupils are equal to the variety of challenges presented by the text. We hope, therefore, to provide teachers with a framework within which they can enable pupils to cope with such challenges.

What we are attempting to do as teachers is to help pupils recognize and understand the sorts of changes which happen both in ourselves as readers and in the texts as we thread our way through them, something which is captured in our quotation from Italo Calvino's fascinating and unusual novel, *If on a Winter's Night a Traveller*. In the novel, the reader is the central character seeking to come to terms with a book which seems to be constantly changing beyond recognition. Significantly, the reader feels impelled to seek out another reader in order to compare responses.

We began the previous chapter by looking at the reading of a pre-reader. By contrast, we want to begin the discussion in this chapter by examining the responses of experienced adult readers to narrative and comparing their reading strategies with Dominic's.

We gave groups of adults the opening pages of three novels: *Remains of the Day* by Kazuo Ishiguro (1989), a recent Booker Prize winner; *London Fields* by Martin Amis (1989), which we chose as an example of a novel which challenges readers in all sorts of ways, not least in terms of its linguistic demands, and *North and South* by Mrs Gaskell (1854/1970), an example of the 'well-written' nineteenth-century novel with a style we thought would be instantly familiar to many of our readers. Our readers came from a variety of backgrounds and ranged in age from twenty to fiftysomething. Before you read the responses of our adult readers, you might like to read the three openings yourself and jot down some initial impressions to each. They are reproduced in the Appendix.

We simply gave the readers a photocopy of each opening on A4 paper and asked them to jot down anything which occurred to them as they read the openings. When we had collected all the material and began to read through it, what struck us very forcibly and, indeed, excited us, was the amazing variety of responses that our readers came up with. The example reproduced below is a typical response.

PICTURES

A frenzied writer pouring over a desk with an old type lamp (don't know why or, i imagined it to be present day) sweating brow etc !!!! gloomy, grim, sinister. a bit typical maybe !!!!!!

SUSPENSE
CONFUSION

This is a true story but I can't believe it's really happening. It's a murder story, too. I can't believe my luck.
And a love story. (I think), of all strange things, so late in the century, so late in the goddamned day.
This is the story of a murder. It hasn't happened yet. But it will. (It had better.) I know the murderer, I know the murderee. I know the time, I know the place. I know the motive (*her* motive) and I know the means. I know who will be the foil, the fool, the poor foal, also utterly destroyed. And I couldn't stop them, I don't think, even if I wanted to. The girl will die. It's what she always wanted. You can't stop people, once they *start*. You can't stop people, once they *start creating*.
What a gift. This page is briefly stained by my tears of gratitude. Novelists don't usually have it so good, do they, when something real happens (something unified, dramatic and pretty saleable), and they just write it down?

Ha Ha!

I must remain calm. I'm on deadline too here, don't forget. Oh, the pregnant agitation. Someone is tickling my heart with delicate fingers. Death is much on people's minds.
Three days ago (is it?) I flew in on a red-eye from New York. I practically had the airplane to myself. I stretched out, calling piteously and frequently to the stewardesses for codeine and cold water. But the red-eye did what a red-eye does. Oh, my. Jesus, I look

i been waiting to... write.?
old?

I have underlined the un't of this understanding.

> writer involved in story
> wants excitement?
'F' alliteration (can't forget the O level training !)
> desperate to be famous ?!!

pretty poetic - not like the rest of the passage. a line to remember.

what's a red-eye? - a plane but what sort? small?

WHAT?
i don't like murder stories usually but i want to know what's going on - where does the author come into it? is he ('i'm presuming it's a he) the murderer ?!

At first we thought that the sheer range of the responses was going to defeat our aim of classifying them into a small number of regularly occurring types. However, eventually, we did manage to sort out two main categories: those responses due to what the reader brings to the text, and those arising from the demands of the text. We also found that we were able to provide further sub-categories on each side of this equation and we will indicate these in the discussion that follows.

Adult readers

So, how did our adult readers respond to the openings of the three novels we had selected? Many of them responded to individual words or longer stretches of text (indeed, whole pages) by seeing a direct reflection of, or allusion to, their own lives. Some of the connections with 'personal life experience' were undoubtedly helpful in forming a rapport with the text. Some responses, however, indicate how far outside the text it is possible to go merely as a result of the personal associations we have for individual words.

A reference to Titania in the opening to *North and South* brought forward the following response from one reader: 'Always reminds me of my starring role in my school days. I played Oberon'. A later reference to Corfu reminded one reader of 'sun, sea, sand, duty frees!' Not, we feel, the kind of response Mrs Gaskell would have expected.

Many readers commented on the nineteenth-century atmosphere apparent in *North and South* and some readers found it hard to relate to the period: 'It seems to me to set the tone for a dated, idealistic, twee and totally unrealistic ramble through a period of time which I cannot and have no inclination to identify with'. This reader hardly seems likely to enjoy the rest of the book. Neither does the reader who wrote, 'The whole thing seems very far removed from the kind of life I lead'. Of course, such readers would probably never have voluntarily chosen such a book to read for themselves. The danger for teachers is that, if we ourselves only read a very narrow range of books, we are hardly going to be enthusiastic about expanding the horizons of our pupils in providing the stimulus for wide reading.

Some personal experiences triggered off by word association can, however, stimulate interest to carry on reading. The opening page of *Remains of the Day* prompted one reader to comment: 'West Country-interest at prospect of his foray into my native land'. But what are we to make of the reader who wrote on her response to the opening of *London Fields*: 'When I am reading my mind is miles away. Thought of the baby buggies at Sea World'.

It seems to us that, to a large extent, we have no control over the kinds of random thoughts that enter our minds as we read a novel. Italo Calvino's advice to the Reader about to begin reading his novel is to: 'Relax. Concentrate. Dispel every other thought. Let the world around you fade'. Is this the kind of advice we would want to offer before every reading? Would our pupils benefit from the advice? Do the extraneous thoughts matter, provided that they don't actually get between us and the text in too obtrusive a way?

In addition to the kinds of personal life experience we have just discussed, we also found that our adult readers made numerous references to what we might term their 'cultural life experience'. Under this heading, we found references to social life in general, cultural references (excluding the literary), assumptions about society and how we live, references to class, gender and age; in short, all the cultural baggage that a reader brings to each text he or she reads. As with our discussion of the personal life references, a few direct quotations from our adult readers will make clear this aspect of response.

One reader's response to the reference to Darlington Hall in *Remains of the Day* was: 'For Darlington Hall I picture a great stately home'. Other readers commented on the setting established at the start of this novel by referring to upper middle class or upper class. The reference to a chaise longue produced the following from one reader:

?elegance
aways conjures up languishing females suffering from 'the vapours'
Barbara Cartland
Pink.

We are not sure if this reader was a man or a woman!

The tone at the opening to *London Fields*, together with references to New York, caused many readers to comment, sometimes disparagingly, about what they perceived as an American novel (we had not told our readers either the titles of the novels or the names of the authors). At the end of the first page of this novel, one reader noted rather sardonically: 'Now we know – frenetic New Yorker. Can I bear the angst?' Another reader made the interesting comment: 'Reading it now in an American accent'. As neither of us is conscious of hearing particular accents when reading silently, we wonder how widespread this particular phenomenon is. The tone of *London Fields* also caused one reader to comment on 'Columbo type musings'.

Some of the most interesting comments within this category reflected the uncertainty of some readers about the meaning of the term 'red-eye'. This response was typical: 'What is a red-eye – I don't like to be made to feel ignorant'. Although we are not experienced members of the transatlantic jetset, we understand the term to refer to those all night crossings which arrive at Heathrow early in the morning leaving the passengers tired, jet-lagged and generally red-eyed.

One set of responses which we found surprising arose from readers who were offended by terms like 'goddamned' and 'Jesus' in *London Fields*: 'The Lord's name in vain, therefore maybe swearing. What is the position of the writer?' Such responses, and we have no idea which age group or sex they came from, illustrate the fact that, although many people would re-gard our society as overwhelmingly secular, the Christian roots within our culture still run very deep.

We deliberately separated general cultural responses from literary ones because literary responses are particularly important in any reading of narra-tive. Some of our adult readers were students on an undergraduate literature course and it might be expected that such readers would be more active in making connections with previous reading. As we found with personal life references, not all the literary responses necessarily take the reader further into the text, but they seem to occur naturally for many people.

Of our three openings, *Remains of the Day* in fact evoked very few literary responses. One reader noted: 'Something in this reminds me of "Brideshead Revisited".' However, the opening of *North and South* con-jured up for many readers memories of Jane Austen. It was as if she was the personification of the nineteenth-century novelist:

> 'imitation' of Jane Austen. Find myself laughing *at* rather than with the au-thor, feels almost as though it could be somebody laughing at Austen. If I knew that this was somebody laughing at Austen I'd be more confident about find-ing the extract funny; as it is I'm not quite sure what to think.

This reader obviously hasn't got the same confidence as Dominic in expres-sing opinions and views without the fear that they may be the wrong kind of response. Our adult reader seems to be searching for the 'correct' response without any certainty of having found it.

The opening to *London Fields* produced a variety of expectations about the kind of novel it was. Many readers thought that the opening couple of lines indicated that it was to be some kind of thriller: 'Murder story? No thanks' was one comment. The line 'It's a murder story' produced re-sponses ranging from: 'Agatha' to 'Ed McBain', and 'sounds American perhaps a trashy murder mystery suspense (Yuk), definitely not P.D. James'. Such comments obviously reflect the range of authors familiar to our readers. Jackie Collins and J.D. Salinger were other writers referred to. This either serves to demonstrate that this is an extremely interesting first page or indicates that, as with the Jane Austen response, once a reader has the writer of a particular genre in mind, all other examples of the genre seem to become the property of this one writer.

Thus far, we have concentrated on the kinds of personal response that relate to the past experiences, readings and lives of our readers triggered by some textual reference. In the previous chapter, we found that this was exactly what happened with three-year-old Dominic when a word or phrase in *A Dark, Dark Tale* recalled a memory of something his grandmother had told him about his dad. These random word associations seem to be an essential component of the reading process right from the early stages.

Between Dominic and our adult readers lie years of experience with different kinds of text, both fiction and non-fiction. The adult has learned to cope with the basic linguistic challenges of most texts, although we feel that part of the resistance to *London Fields* was due to the demands it makes on our linguistic competence. We have also, as adults, acquired a literary competence which, at its basic level, means that we know what we like and we like what we know.

As a consequence, when we come across a text that challenges this competence, we have two options. We can either struggle on and add to our repertoire of literary and linguistic skills or, as many of our adults indicated, we can give up and stick with what we feel most comfortable with. The challenge for the teachers of Dominic, Kyle and Thomas – our three pre-readers in the last chapter – lies in constantly dripfeeding them at school with a wide variety of texts so that they don't get 'hooked' too early on one particular genre to the exclusion of all others. We have all encountered the reader at primary school who will only read school stories or Enid Blyton or Roald Dahl. Sometimes it is a hopeless task trying to move them on to something else.

Summarizing the responses of the adult readers, we feel that it was clear that there were as many readings as there were readers and an author has no way of knowing how the individual reader is going to react. As Natalie Babbitt (1991) expresses it: 'A book, once it is published, takes on a sort of chameleon-like character. It becomes something different for each person who reads it, and who's to say one of these interpretations is more valid than anothers'. It therefore seems to be important for all teachers to encourage children to discuss stories in a personal way in order to demonstrate that each of us has some experience or knowledge that can add to the richness of everybody else's enjoyment of the text. It is not always the pupil getting the 'right' answer to the closed question about a text who has most to offer.

The text

In this section, we turn from the personal responses of the reader to examine some of the ways in which narratives make their own characteristic demands on us. Our aim is to show that readers must not only rely on the kinds of experience we discussed in the previous section, but must also be aware of textual conventions. The importance of such conventions is stressed by Selden (1989):

> A text or piece of text could be made to mean many different things by different readers. Literary texts are more likely to give rise to variable interpretation than non-literary texts . . . However, this does not mean that interpretation is therefore completely subjective and impressionistic because . . . interpretations are produced within a set of rules or conventions.

Much of our discussion about the text side of reading will focus on the sorts of features that might be included under such a 'set of rules'.

One set of rules involves the *linguistic structure* of the book and such a structure will present a variety of challenges depending on the kind of linguistic competence we bring to it. Under this umbrella term, we have included a variety of features including, for instance, the different sentence patterns an author uses. Such patterns will vary according to the stylistic effect being aimed at. As readers we have to learn to be sensitive to subtle variations in the syntax. As one reader noted about *London Fields:* 'I like the really short sentences'. Short, staccato sentences can help a writer to suggest dramatic tension, whereas longer sentences are often employed in descriptive passages in which a series of subordinate clauses are joined onto the main clause. The opening page of *Remains of the Day* is littered with examples of such complex sentences:

> The idea of such a journey came about, I should point out, from a most kind suggestion put to me by Mr. Farraday himself one afternoon almost a fortnight ago, when I had been dusting the portraits in the library.

It is quite a feat actually picking out the main clause in this sentence ('I should point out') from the series of subordinate clauses. The complexity of this and similar sentences give the whole page a pedantic, plodding tone which helps to reflect the character of the narrator, Stevens. One of our readers commented: 'Pompous, longwinded language'.

A second area we would include under the heading linguistic structure is that related to meaning (*semantics*). We have already discussed in the previous chapter the difference between the denotative or dictionary meaning of a word and the associative or subjective meaning words can have. All writers use both types of meaning and, as readers, we have to be able to be sensitive enough to pick up on subtle nuances. It can have some unusual and unintended results. Several of our readers commented that the phrase 'calling piteously' in *London Fields* suggested that the author was male. The inference was correct, but what is particularly male about this phrase, we wonder?

In considering linguistic structure, we also need to take into account the process by which the jumble of graphemes, morphemes, words, phrases, sentences, meanings and references becomes a text. The following quotation from Fowler (1986) indicates just what it is that is included in the term 'text':

> Sentences are linked together by an intricate system of cohesive ties. Textual cohesion distinguishes a well-formed text from a random list of sentences. A cohesive text stays on its topic or makes clear shifts of topic, develops a subject rationally and indicates what are the prominent and the subordinate parts of an argument or story.

We think that developing children's recognition of cohesion and stressing its importance in their own writing is something worth spending time on. The following is a simple example to illustrate just what cohesive ties are and how they help to make a collection of sentences into a text.

Let's look at the second and third sentences in *North and South*:

> But as Margaret half suspected, Edith had fallen asleep. She lay curled up on the sofa in the back drawing-room in Harley Street, looking very lovely in her white muslin and blue ribbon.

In the second sentence, the two pronouns 'she' and 'her' refer back to Edith and act as cohesive ties in binding the two sentences together.

A more complex example of the importance of cohesion can be found on the opening page of one of the novels we used with our primary readers, *The Eighteenth Emergency*. As you read the following passage, note the number of times the definite article is used:

> The pigeons flew out of the alley in one long swoop and settled on the awning of the grocery store. A dog ran out of the alley with a torn Cracker Jack box in his mouth. Then came the boy.
>
> The boy was running hard and fast. He stopped at the sidewalk, looked both ways, saw that the street was deserted and kept going. The dog caught the boy's fear, and he started running with him.
>
> The two of them ran together for a block. The dog's legs were so short he appeared to be on wheels. His Cracker Jack box was hitting the sidewalk. He kept glancing at the boy because he didn't know why they were running. The boy knew. He did not even notice the dog beside him or the trail of spilled Cracker Jacks beind.
>
> Suddenly the boy slowed down, went up some steps and entered an apartment building. The dog stopped. He sensed that the danger had passed, but he stood for a moment at the bottom of the steps. Then he went back to eat the Cracker Jacks scattered on the sidewalk and to snarl at the pigeons who had flown down to get some.
>
> Inside the building the boy was still running. He went up the stairs three at a time, stumbled, pulled . . .

Once you are looking out for it, the use of 'the' is quite intrusive in this passage, isn't it? One of the functions of the definite article in English is to refer back to something already mentioned in a passage (anaphoric reference). A straightforward example occurs in the opening paragraph of the above passage. In paragraph one, 'a dog' is mentioned. After this reference, the reader knows that all future references to 'the dog' are anaphorically referring to the same dog. The passage thus acquires cohesion.

However, in the first paragraph of *The Eighteenth Emergency*, there are references to 'the pigeons', 'the alley', 'the awning of the grocery store'. None of these things have previously been mentioned, so there is no question of anaphoric reference. We would suggest that the author uses the definite article here for a completely different purpose. She seems to be pointing to different features in the scene she is describing and the effect is to draw the reader right into it, so that we clearly visualize and vicariously experience what is happening. The division between reader and text appears to dissolve and there is a feeling of a shared world and a consciousness of our orientation in it. Before the end of the first page, we have been drawn into the story and are 'hooked'.

We can do useful work in the classroom on cohesion. One way in is to ask children to find examples of pronouns and explain which characters they refer to. If they find it difficult to sort out the differences we can ask them to go through a page of text (photocopied), ringing round the references to the various characters in a story in different coloured pens. The first time a character is mentioned we are, of course, usually given the name, and this provides an easy starting point. This sort of exercise helps to emphasize how important it is for writers to make it easy for readers to distinguish between characters. It also provides an insight into the craft of writing.

In addition to the linguistic structure of the text, there is also the important question of the narrative structure to consider, a term which includes intertextuality, extratextuality, story and narrative process. *Intertextuality* refers to the way in which one text makes reference to another either by direct quote or paraphrase. The more developed our own literary competence, the more sensitive we are likely to be to recognize such allusions. The reference to Shakespeare's Titania in *North and South* puzzled some of our readers who asked the question: 'Who is Titania?'

Extratextuality includes all the extraneous cultural knowledge assumed by the text. Clearly, there is a close link between this area and our personal cultural experiences. The key issue once again is whether there is a close match between our cultural experience and that assumed by the text. Clearly, the older a novel is, the more difficult it will be for us to pick up on the kinds of everyday cultural knowledge assumed by the text. But it is not only older novels that can cause problems. The reference to the 'red-eye' in *London Fields* puzzled nearly all our readers.

The most familiar term in referring to narrative structure is plainly 'story'. By story we mean WHAT happens? WHO to? WHERE does it take place? WHEN? One or more of these features will appear on the opening page of a novel. Many of the questions raised by both our adult and young readers related to speculations about the WHO and the WHAT of the narrative.

Most children who have had stories read to them before they come to school will already have cottoned on to the fact that this is how stories 'work' and will have begun to use the knowledge in creating their own narratives. We have already seen a lovely example from Thomas in Chapter 2. However, we have also come across children who have no idea of what storying is all about and their number appears to be on the increase. On the reception teacher falls the burden of trying to compensate for what is missing by reading as many stories as possible during the day.

Our final term, *narrative process*, is meant to suggest the means used by the author to tell the story. Within this broad term we include such details as the agent who tells the story, for example the narrator or implied author, and the point of view from which the story is told.

In terms of the responses from our adults and young readers, we were not surprised that the latter did not indicate any awareness of the difference between the real author and the person telling the story, but what did surprise us in view of the fact that some of our adult readers were English undergraduates was their complete inability to distinguish between them.

A large number of comments were made about the narrator in *London Fields*. In view of the fact that the story is a first person narrative and that first person is supposedly the novelist himself who is going to witness (or commit?) a murder, this might have been expected. However, what was surprising was that our readers all seemed to think that the author in the narrative was Martin Amis and not an implied author created by the real one for a particular creative purpose. This inability to distinguish fact from fiction is conveyed by one of our readers who, next to the line 'Novelists don't usually have it so good, do they, when something real happens?', then wrote, 'impossible to do if it's real – could be done for not telling the police in advance'. The reader obviously knows this is fiction but there is a note of uncertainty in the comment.

Next to the exclamation 'what a gift' by the implied author in welcoming a ready-made plot for a novel, one reader noted: 'Is writing usually hard work for the writer?' Similarly, many readers seemed unable to recognize the point of view from which the narrative was being told and did not realize that resisting the untrustworthy narrator, particularly the first person narrator, is all part of the reading process. Only one reader seemed aware of the manipulative process which can be involved and this reader rather resented it: 'I felt like I was being dangled on a piece of string – not being invited or gently persuaded to come into the novel and perhaps identify with a character – more of the opposite really'.

We are sure that teachers at primary level can indicate to their pupils the difference between the real writer and the one who appears to be telling the story. Stories are, after all, 'made up'.

Reader/text interaction

So far, we have separated the reader from the text in quite an arbitrary way. There does, of course, have to be an interaction between the two, and we want now to discuss the nature of this interaction. What follows owes much to the influential work of Wolfgang Iser and what has become known as Reader Response Theory. Iser argued that as we engage with a narrative text we form expectations about what is going to happen next or who it might involve. Expectations can begin, though, before we even open a book. The picture on the cover, the name of the author, the very smell of the new, unopened pages, or the account of the story in the blurb can all stimulate excitement and a desire to get started on the actual reading.

The expectations or predictions that we make as we start to read the text itself are constantly being modified in the light of our engagement with the text. During our work with adult readers we found that, although we only gave them the opening pages of novels to read, expectations or predictions were an important aspect of the responses of a considerable number. They were often in the form of questions that the readers wanted answering:

> wanted to read on – was intrigued by the style/approach
> who is the writer?
> how is he/she involved?
> must know other people involved well to be able to predict?
> what is going to happen?

wrote one reader at the end of the first page of *London Fields*. Another reader posed a different series of questions about the novel:

> What is the writer's part in the murder?
> Who is the girl?
> Is the writer at the centre?

In raising these questions, the readers seem to be posing issues which they see as at the centre of the text and which will have to be answered if a satisfactory reading is to be obtained. Thus, one reader commented about *London Fields*: 'Sets no questions which I would like answered'.

Some readers were not sure at the end of the opening page whether the issues or characters introduced were in fact going to be central to a novel. One of our readers wondered at the end of the first page of *North and South*: 'Is the novel going to be about Edith or Margaret?' However, a minority of our readers were able to make confident predictions about the outcomes of two of the novels even on the evidence of a single page. On *North and South* one adult commented: 'I'm sure Margaret will meet Mr. Right and live happily ever after'. And *Remains of the Day* elicited the following: 'Seems that whatever is going to happen in the novel happens to Stevens (the employee) whilst the employer is away in U.S.A. – want to read on to find out where he goes, what he does etc.'

As a result of the sorts of questions that the openings to the novels raised, quite a number of readers had formed strong enough feelings about the narratives to make a judgement about them which determined whether they would carry on reading beyond the first page. 'This is the biggest load of rubbish I've read for ages', commented one reader about *London Fields*. Another reader also felt strong antipathy to the book: 'American third rate drivel and an insult to my intelligence!!'

Such comments throw a fascinating light on the low tolerance of some readers towards anything that is slightly different from their expectations of what a novel should be like. The comments also indicate the variety of responses a single narrative is likely to produce. Not all our readers formed the antipathy to *London Fields* indicated above: 'I'm going rushing down the page – I want to read it', claimed one reader excitedly. Generally, though, there was some resistance to reading further with this novel. One reader even communicated his feelings for the author: 'Generally gives an antipathy to the author wouldn't like her/him'.

The other novels did not arouse such strong pro and anti feelings although, again, some readers expressed views about whether they would carry on reading the rest of the novel: 'Would certainly like to read more. My sort of holiday reading', commented one reader about *North and South*. Some readers found the style of *Remains of the Day* a barrier to their wanting to read on: 'If this style continued would probably find the novel difficult to finish – doesn't flow'.

One result, then, of the reader/text interaction seems to be the rapid development of feelings of antipathy or liking for a text which leads to a decision about whether it is worth carrying on. We wonder how many decisions made in the shops of airports have been regretted once the first few pages of a chosen novel have been read?

Possibly the most powerful aspect of the interaction between the reader and the text is the way many (possibly most) readers form images of scenes or characters as a way of orientating themselves *vis-à-vis* the text. These images are often very clear and sharply defined and become our fixed idea of what a character or scene looks like. Who has not experienced a feeling of disappointment at seeing a film version of a favourite book because the director's vision has not been the same as ours?

One feature of our respondents was that only a small minority noted any clear pictures as a result of reading the opening page of *London Fields*, although it did produce the following interesting comment:

> I pictured someone (most likely a man) sitting talking with me. At the same time I was picturing in my mind what could happen later. I was seeing what could be happening later on. I was always the friend of the author. He was standing next to me seeing it with me. But still just talking with me. Like when someone is telling you a story.

Both *North and South* and *Remains of the Day* were responsible for a greater number of examples of image-forming. Some of the images are very detailed and not only describe what the reader sees but also the viewpoint from which the scene is observed. Here is a good example from *North and South*:

> . . . mental picture – I am *standing* in the room, looking down at Edith. Black curly hair, ribbons, with a young face. The room is fairly dark – not a particularly *vivid* image, the only furniture that stands out is the settee which Edith is resting on – fairly old, with a flowery design and mahogany armsides. There is also a brass lamp to the side.

What an amazingly detailed description and it's also interesting to find examples where an image triggered off by a word or phrase can take off on a life of its own, as the next example from *Remains of the Day* illustrates:

> Here, I can picture a car – black, shiny, old fashioned, driving along country lanes, surrounded by green fields and 'English countryside'. I am viewing this scene from a distance almost as though from a bird's eye view.

The following reader also went outside the frame within which the opening to *North and South* takes place:

> Image formed – two women one on settee other standing over her. I don't see the whole room and contents but I see the door as heavy and made of dark wood which leads to a panelled hall – this I think is due to the reference to there being a 'buzz' in the next room so I extend my image to beyond the room where the two women are. I have no part in the image but am perhaps something like a T.V. camera in a room – always viewing from the same angle.

The final sentence in this extract is fascinating in indicating that it is not necessary for the reader to be an animate observer of the scene – it is also possible to be something inanimate like a camera.

Picturing appears to be one of the main means by which the reader closes the gaps which are inevitably left by the author in the text. We are never told everything about a character or a scene – there are always bits missing. However, our psychological need to fill gaps means that we can finish the task that the author has only partly completed.

Iser pointed to the dynamic relationship between reader and text. Until the reader picks up a book and starts to read, there is just a mass of black marks on white paper. Once the reader starts predicting, questioning and picturing, however, the dynamic process is set in motion, bringing the text to life. It is part of our task as teachers to help our pupils engage with texts by providing them with activities that assist in this dynamic process to ensure a richer experience of reading.

Children's responses

When we worked with a class of primary pupils, we made exactly the same request as we gave to our adults: 'Write down anything that comes into your head as you read the openings'. We used the openings of novels we judged to be typical of those aimed at the year 6 age range and they were given to the pupils on A3 photocopies. The novels were: *The Eighteenth Emergency* (Betsy Byars 1973), *Run for Your Life* (David Line 1970), *The Worst Witch* (Jill Murphy 1978) and *The Way to Sattin Shore* (Philippa Pearce 1985). As with the openings to the adult novels, all the first pages are reproduced in the Appendix.

One feature that immediately differentiated the children's responses from the adults' was that the children wrote very little. It may well have been the case that the children we worked with were unused to such an open-ended task. They were possibly more used to reading a passage and then answering a series of closed questions designed to test 'comprehension'. Despite this, however, it still proved possible to categorize the responses under the same headings as for the adults.

Under the personal life heading, there were very few comments by the children. In fact, only two responses could be regarded as falling into the category. One pupil wrote 'Paula's dog' next to the references to the dog in *The Eighteenth Emergency*, and another pupil wrote down comments that indicated that he had the same problem of wandering attention that some of our adult respondents had. Thus, he commented:

> Wonder what I have got for lunch?
> Don't want to go swimming
> People talking in the class,

round the opening page of *Run for Your Life*.

One or two pupils did respond by making an imaginative leap into the situation they were reading. This example illustrates a pupil doing this after reading *The Worst Witch*: 'It must be horrible up in the school'. This is not quite the same as personal life experience but could be regarded as the pupil vicariously experiencing the fictional account or imposing her own feelings on the situation.

There was a similar dearth of references under the cultural life experience category. One child noted 'American' against *The Eighteenth Emergency*.

We can only speculate as to why there should have been so few references under these categories, which were so fruitful an area for our adult readers. Surely a great part of the enjoyment of reading a novel comes from forming links between the text and our everyday experiences? Perhaps we need, as teachers, to indicate much more clearly the kinds of response that are possible, so pupils see that it is a natural part of reading to make links with books and the 'real' world. It can't be the case, we believe, that none of the children we worked with don't make these kinds of links. It is far more likely that they considered them not the kinds of response that form a legitimate part of the reading curriculum. How sad if they have to relearn a skill which, as Dominic so clearly demonstrates, they probably had before they even came to school.

It was a similar depressing story under the literary experience heading. One pupil noted, 'It's a bit like *The Lion, The Witch and the Wardrobe*', after reading the opening page but this was the solitary response under this heading.

Some pupils responded to the texts by providing brief summaries (sometimes single words) of paragraphs or sections and this seemed to be a way of recording the fact that they had understood some part of the text. One reader, for example, had underlined two sentences in *The Worst Witch* and noted: 'Those words tell me it is like a haunted (house)'. Another reader wrote just four words round *Run for Your Life*. 'Lonely' next to the opening lines; 'dirty' half way down; 'bullying' a bit lower down; and 'mysterious' at the bottom. The first three are certainly summaries of what happens on the opening page and indicate that the reader has comprehended the text on one level (the level needed to indicate to external examiners that she can read?).

One pupil drew a map of the house after reading *The Way to Sattin Shore*. Was this to reassure herself that she had understood the text sufficiently to have a clear picture of the inside of the house? Other pupils wrote short summarizing words and phrases and sometimes drew inferences from what they had read. For instance, one pupil thought, 'It looks like she doesn't really look forward to going home', about Kate Tranter. Another pupil's summary of *The Worst Witch*, 'The school was on a mountain surrounded by a pine forest', was also followed by the judgement: 'It should not finish in the middle of a sentence'. The first page had ended in the middle of a sentence and obviously we should have printed the first part of the second page to ensure grammatical correctness!

Another pupil made the inference that the Tranter family were 'poor because they keep the electricity off'.

The pupils we worked with were much more confident when it came to recording the kinds of judgements, expectations, pictures and questions we discussed above as occurring for many readers as a result of the interaction with text. Questions which occurred to our primary readers arose from various texts. 'Why a church yard?', wondered one pupil about the opening of *The Way to Sattin Shore*. 'Is anybody in?', asked another about the same story. One pupil who read *The Eighteenth Emergency* asked: 'Why is the boy running?' For those of you who know this story, the question relates directly to the central theme of the whole book. The boy (Mouse) does not stop running, metaphorically speaking, until the final chapter. A number of the readers also felt able to predict what they thought a particular story was going to be about. 'I think it is going to be about the school and the girl', thought one reader about *The Worst Witch*. Another reader wrote: 'I think it's going to be about a witch'.

The most interesting part of the interaction was the nature of the pictures which were conjured up by the different openings. The pupils either tried to record their responses in words or by drawing an image of what they saw. Printed opposite is a drawing of the 'dark side of the moon', which was how one pupil responded to the chapter heading 'The Beam of Darkness' from *The Way to Sattin Shore*. Other pupils scattered drawings of articles and objects referred to in various opening pages. Were these the sorts of activities pupils were more familiar with in the classroom – descriptions followed by illustrations?

Another response, this time written, indicates how some words or phrases or, as in this case, a complete sentence, can evoke strong feelings or emotions in readers. The pupil underlined the following sentence from *The Worst Witch*: 'at the top of a high mountain surrounded by a pine forest', and written above it, 'it is kind of creepy like mist half hid the school'. This written response was also accompanied by a drawing of the scene. Obviously, this part-sentence had a powerful effect on the pupil. A second pupil also responded to the atmosphere of the opening page of this story by writing: 'It is like a mountain with a castle and the castle is really like a haunted castle and the castle is full of witches'.

None of our readers reported whether they wanted to read on any further with any of the stories, although there were one or two claims that stories were, in those words of ultimate judgement for many children today, 'boring' or even 'boaring'.

It is now possible to summarize the discussion in this chapter by providing a model which indicates on the left-hand side the responses of the readers as we have discussed them and, on the right-hand side, the demands of the text. In the middle is the meeting point between reader and

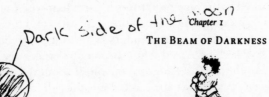

Chapter 1

THE BEAM OF DARKNESS

Here is Kate Tranter coming home from school in the
January dusk – the first to come, because she is the
youngest of her family. Past the churchyard. Past
the shops. Along the fronts of the tall, narrow terrace
houses she goes. Not this one, nor this one, nor this ...

Stop at the house with no lit window.

This is home.

Up three steps to the front door, and feel for the key
on the string in her pocket. Unlock, and then in. Stand
just inside the door with the door now closed, at her back.

Stand so, in the hall. Ahead, to the right, the stairs.
Ahead, to the left, the passage to the kitchen: in the wider
part, by the back door, a round, red, friendly eye has seen
her – the reflector of her bicycle.

To the left of the hall, Granny's room.

Kate Tranter took a slow breath. She made herself ready
to start across the floor to the stairs – to cross the dark
beam that came from her grandmother's room through
the gap where her grandmother's door stood ajar.

On a weekday, at this time, her grandmother's eyes
were always turned to that door, as she sat in her room

Granmas
Room

TEXT AS 'LIFE'

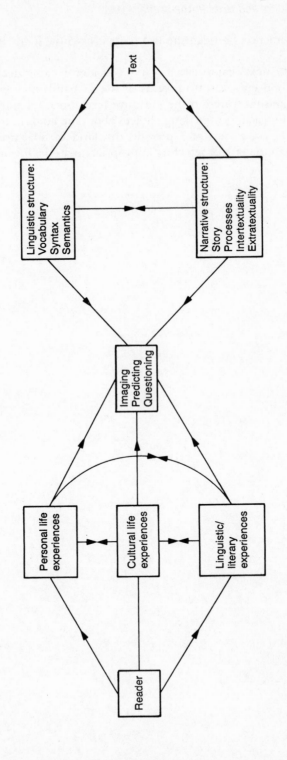

TEXT AS ARTEFACT

text. Interaction between the two parts is essential if any real ending is to take place.

In the next chapter, we go on to consider in closer detail the openings of two children's novels in terms of the demands they make on readers both linguistically and at the narrative level. Such an analysis will, we believe, help teachers in making choices about the kinds of text to introduce into their classrooms and provide the kind of analytical data to help teachers in the task of selecting appropriate material for individual pupils.

CHAPTER 4

Reading into writing

In narrative the 'literary' is that which tantalises without being either too obvious or absurdly unpredictable.

(Stibbs, 'The teacherly practice of literary theory', 1993)

Evidence (eg by Eckhoff) suggests that children tend to write in the style of the books they are currently reading.

(Perara, 'The good book: linguistic aspects', 1993)

In the previous chapter, we examined in some detail the responses of readers to narrative texts and also the kinds of demands made on readers by such texts. As we saw, it is an extremely complex process. We must stress again that, though we separated the component parts of the process, the interaction between the two sides occurs almost simultaneously as we engage with the text.

We thought it would be interesting to subject some narratives written for children to the sort of analysis we used in the previous chapter in order to discover whether the same kinds of complexity are at work as in adult fiction. We have already discussed the issue of cohesion within the context of *The Eighteenth Emergency* and found that children's writers use the same kinds of sophisticated stylistic features as adult writers.

We chose two texts to analyse, using the opening pages for our purposes as before. The first opening was from Enid Blyton's (1973) story, *The Naughtiest Girl in the School*. Although she has endured much adverse criticism about the sexism, classism and every other kind of -ism, Blyton remains a firm favourite with thousands of primary children. Angel Scott (1993) indicates why:

The stories offer a predictable world where the reader knows what is going to happen but the creation of the atmosphere and the power of the narrative still sustain the reader's interest and excitement.

The second text was from Alan Garner's (1965) novel *Elidor*. Garner is at the end of the critical spectrum to Blyton, and his writing represents what many people would consider 'good' literature. You will find the two extracts in the Appendix and we would like you to read them both before continuing the rest of the discussion.

We were also intrigued to discover how far the writing of a year 6 pupil made use of the same techniques as a professional writer and, following the discussion in this chapter of the work of two professionals, we discuss a piece of narrative by ten-year-old Chris, using exactly the same framework.

Enid Blyton and Alan Garner

The discussion about the two openings will follow the same format as in the last chapter. That is, we will use two headings – linguistic structure and narrative structure – in order to isolate characteristic features of each text.

Linguistic structure

The discussion below will centre on differences in vocabulary in instances where we feel that there are significant stylistic effects achieved by the use of particular nouns or adjectives or other parts of speech. Another area will be to compare the vocabulary in terms of the denotative and connotative meanings attached to words. We also want to consider the variety of sentence structures used in the two passages to pinpoint any important differences which might affect their readability. A final task will be to discuss both passages in terms of their use of cohesive ties.

As we mentioned above, we chose examples of text from these two authors because they seemed to us to stand at opposing ends of the perceived value scale as far as children's literature is concerned. Blyton is one of the most popular writers, if not *the* most popular writer, this century in Great Britain and yet she is increasingly attacked from all sorts of directions for her baleful influence on children. Alan Garner has won awards for his writing and has established a reputation for quality writing with an appeal that extends beyond the years of childhood.

One surprising feature of the two texts we looked at is that, judged purely on a level of linguistic difficulty, it is hard to detect which presents most challenge to the reader. That the Garner passage is more difficult we hope to demonstrate later, but the fact that, linguistically, there is little surface difference serves to remind us that reading is not just a matter of decoding. Difficulties and challenges in texts lie not only in the linguistic structure but at deeper levels which only those readers who have wide and developing experience of different varieties of books will have access to.

In fact, even a brief study of the vocabulary used by Garner and Blyton suggests that neither makes particularly hard demands on the reader. Both openings make extensive use of dialogue, but the vocabulary within the dialogue is fairly formal. Garner uses some colloquialisms such as 'fed up' and 'chucked off', but there is little attempt to capture the Mancunian dialect. The vocabulary in *Elidor* is in fact very spare and lean. Garner uses few adjectives except to give very precise information about an object. For example: 'It was a tall machine of squares and wheels and lighted panels'. Similarly, Blyton makes few demands on the level of vocabulary.

One difference between the passages is worth pointing out. Notice the numbers of adjectives used in the Blyton extract: 'spoilt', 'naughty', 'silly', 'lovely', 'pretty', 'blue', 'fair', 'obedient', 'good-mannered'. What is the effect of these adjectives? We would suggest that they fill in details which save the reader from a lot of work in filling the gaps that a writer like Garner leaves for his reader. In other words, Blyton provides her readers with an easier read not by leaving out words but by putting more in. They might make greater demand in the physical sense of giving the reader more to read, but they leave the reader with less mental work to do. This use of adjectives also enables her to guide or push the reader into a certain point of view from which to read the story. Who can resist the notion of the pretty blue-eyed rascal? It is difficult to read against the text when the writer does this kind of thing. We find that even on the first page of the book we are on the side of the naughtiest girl on the block.

In passing, we might also question whether the notions of obedience and good manners put forward by Mrs Allen to Elizabeth are really what education is all about!

The use of verbs in *Elidor* is interesting in suggesting differences between the characters who appear on the opening page. Until Roland makes an appearance towards the bottom of the page, all the characters either 'say' or 'sit'. Roland, however, 'drives' the street map and 'spun' the wheel – these are much more dynamic words which suggest real activity, and a sense of control which is absent from the kind of directionless conversation which has preceded Roland's appearance. Does the difference here denote something important about who the book is going to be about? Possibly, but you would have to be a skilled reader to pick up this kind of clue.

There are few words in either passage from specialist registers that might cause the competent reader any problem. The word 'sculptor' perhaps in Garner and the term 'governess' in Blyton. This is probably more a question of cultural experience, but in the 1990s is the concept of governess one that is likely to be fully understood by the majority of readers, even where the audience is familiar with, and enthusiastic for, Enid Blyton?

The use of inquit tags (words like 'said', etc.) is worth drawing attention to in both passages. Garner uses an unchanging 'said' between stretches of speech, which helps to emphasize the lack of any activity on the first page until the appearance of Roland. Blyton does, too, on the whole, save for two instances. Mrs Allen speaks 'sternly' at one point and Elizabeth 'giggled' as she speaks at another. These examples are again revealing in indicating the control exercised by the authorial voice of Enid Blyton. Isn't she really telling her readers where their sympathies should lie? Would the implied reader sympathize with the 'stern' parent?

In terms of sentence structure, there are 32 sentences on the opening page of *Elidor*, consisting of 256 words, an average of eight per sentence. The longest sentence is 24 words long, and the shortest is one. In *The Naughtiest Girl in the School*, there are 22 sentences, 278 words at an average of 12½ words per sentence. The longest sentence is 35 words long and the shortest is two. These figures are revealing in pointing out that sentence length is not necessarily a real determiner of the difficulty of a text, although longer sentences may well provide slower readers with more opportunities for running out of steam and forgetting the beginning before they reach the end.

Both openings use a variety of sentence types, though there are no imperatives in the Blyton text. There are examples of simple sentences in both:

They sat on the bench behind the statue of Watt.

(*Elidor*)

Elizabeth giggled.

(*The Naughtiest Girl in the School*)

The Blyton passage does not use any compound sentences (two or more simple sentences joined by conjunctions such as 'and' or 'but'), as in the following from *Elidor*: 'Roland spun a wheel at the side of the map, and the index whirled round, a blur under the glass'.

Both texts use a large number of complex sentences. A complex sentence is one in which a main clause is connected to one or more subordinate clauses, typically by words such as 'when', 'because', 'if', 'so', 'that', 'which' and 'although'. The most complex sentence both in terms of its structure and readability is the following from *The Naughtiest Girl in the School:* 'You are spoilt and naughty, and although daddy and I were going to leave you here with Miss Scott, when we went away, I think it would be better for you to go to school'. Considering this is a piece of dialogue, it is an extremely complex construction. Basically, it is a compound–complex sentence consisting of two main clauses: 'You are spoilt and naughty' and 'I think it would be better for you to go to school' joined by the first 'and' in the sentence. There are three subordinate clauses, one beginning with 'although' ('although daddy and I were going to leave you here with Miss

Scott'), a second clause beginning with 'when' ('when we went away') and a third following 'I think', where we could add 'that' to complete the clause: 'I think that it would be better for you to go to school'.

In addition to the examples we have discussed above, there are a few examples of minor sentences in both passages (that is, sentences that are structurally incomplete, with a verb or subject or other constituent left out). This is perhaps surprising in view of the fact that over half of each opening is taken up with dialogue and most of us, we would bet, do not speak in perfectly formed sentences. This is not unusual in the dialogue of novels where most characters tend to use complete sentences.

Try reading both passages out loud. Do the conversations sound natural? We would suggest they don't. As Lennard Davis (1987) explains: 'most people will perceive conversations in novels as simply a transplantation – with changes to be sure – of ordinary speech. But . . . dialogue in novels looks actually nothing at all like conversation in real life.' He goes on to point out:

> . . . when novelists reproduce only the verbal signs of conversation they are chang-
> ing dramatically the nature of the act. They are universalizing the particular
> moment and, more important, robbing it of its interactive, face-to-face quality.

Thus, we miss the falling and rising intonation patterns which carry so much of the meaning in face-to-face dialogue. This is one area where the novelist often has to leave gaps for us to fill ourselves and many readers supply an internal voice which provides the missing intonation. Writers will often help us of course. As we have already seen, Enid Blyton's Mrs Allen speaks 'sternly' at one point. No such adverbial support occurs in *Elidor*, at least on the opening page.

Conversations in novels are also noticeably free of the hesitations, pauses, back-tracking, repetitions and body language with which real conversations are filled. Perhaps this is one reason why so many readers create visual images to fill these voids.

When we examine the cohesive ties involving pronouns, it is also clear who the main character is in the Blyton passage. In the opening 28 lines of *The Naughtiest Girl in the School*, there are 40 references either directly to Elizabeth or to a pronominal substitute. This device not only makes the passage very cohesive, it implants very firmly in our minds the notion of who is important. Garner, too, uses personal pronouns as a device to ensure textual cohesiveness, but there is nowhere near the same emphasis on a single character.

Narrative structure

So much then for the linguistic structure of the passages. We want to emphasize again the point that the notion of a 'difficult' novel may arise from features other than the linguistic. Once we can read competently, the vocabulary and syntax are not usually a real problem. The problems lie within features of the narrative structure of the novel and this is where we need to look to discover the real differences between Enid Blyton and Alan Garner.

The basic narrative framework is, in fact, similar in both *Elidor* and *The Naughtiest Girl in the School*. We find out something about the WHO of the story, though it is by no means clear by the end of the first page of *Elidor* who will emerge as the principal character. Will it be Nicholas, for example, who appears to be the leader? We also find out something about the WHERE in Blyton – we will shortly move from Elizabeth's house to a boarding school. Already, readers familiar with the genre will be getting a comfortable feeling; they know what sort of a book they are dealing with. We are not really given any clues in Garner. The children are restless; moving home is mentioned and a street map seems to offer endless scope for places to escape to.

Similarly, Garner provides us with few clues about the WHAT, whereas references to naughty girls in school leave us with little doubt about what Elizabeth is going to get up to, although we are not given any hint of the resolution, of course. Finally, notions of WHEN are vague in both books. Both are probably set in some kind of non-specific 'present', although we might speculate as to whether there are still governesses in gainful employment.

In terms of story orientation, the two children's novels are very similar to the adult openings where readers are also given information about character, place, plot and time. Amis even tells us 'this is a murder story' in the opening lines of *London Fields* (though whether this particular narrator is to be trusted is another matter).

To summarize the difference in story orientation between Garner and Blyton we can point to the fact that, once again, it is a case of Blyton locating her readers much more securely in a particular environment: we know where we are going, who it will involve and what will happen. These features are much less clear in *Editor*. No doubt, some readers will already have decided not to continue the journey – they may be feeling slightly disorientated. If their motives are merely to seek an easy, relaxing read, such challenges as those provided by Garner will already have them shifting uncomfortably in their chairs.

If we look at the openings of *The Naughtiest Girl in the School* and *Elidor* in terms of the kinds of cultural assumptions they make (extratextuality), Garner assumes a knowledge of folksy sayings which would help the reader complete the chapter title 'Thursday's Child' with 'has far to go', suggesting that there will be many stages to go through before the 'child' (whoever it is) and the reader reach the end of the story. The reader will need to be patient! The Garner opening also assumes that references to James Watt and sculptors, although probably not important to the development of the story, might be picked up.

Underpinning the whole of the Blyton passage is the notion of children of well-to-do parents who don't have to go to school and are brought up by governesses. If they do go to school, then it will be a boarding school. Although this kind of cultural reference will no doubt be outside the experience of most readers, there is a long tradition of school stories, it is a distinct genre with its own rules and conventions which are very familiar to most readers. They know what to expect even if the real world of the boarding school is outside their experience.

We are not really sure by the end of the first page of *Elidor* what kind of a story it is going to be. It could be about moving house, and certainly journeys are inferred in the chapter heading, which also suggests a long journey. It could even be about a gang of kids getting into trouble around the streets of Manchester! Each part of the conversation has to be carefully scanned for clues. At this stage, we have to trust the author and be prepared for diversions along the way.

As far as intertextuality is concerned, there is only one reference to another literary work in our two openings and that appears in the epigraph to *Elidor* in the form of a quotation from *King Lear*. Again, it needs a skilled reader to make connections between 'Child Rowland' and the Roland who appears in *Elidor*. But for the reader who does notice the reference, it is a clue that the story is in fact going to focus on Roland.

In our discussion of the textual structure of the adult novels, we pointed out how few of our readers picked up on what we have referred to as the narrative process, part of which involves the voice which tells the story. Notice how the narrator in Blyton is much more intrusive and omniscient than the quieter voice in *Elidor*. The narrator in *The Naughtiest Girl in the School* not only provides great detail about Elizabeth, but creates a point of view from which we will read the story. Aren't we intended to feel sympathetic towards Elizabeth rather than 'stern' mummy and 'silly' Miss Scott? Thus Blyton saves her readers the trouble of even having to make up their minds about where their sympathies lie.

We can summarize the differences between these two passages by thinking in terms of the *implied reader* assumed by the narratives. The implied reader of *Elidor* is one who has read many different kinds of narrative, who is prepared to be patient by not expecting everything to be explained in the first few lines. This reader will pick up linguistic clues as to the relative importance of the various characters and the setting of the novel. The implied reader of *Elidor* will also not expect the details of the plot to be immediately apparent on the opening page.

The implied reader of *The Naughtiest Girl in the School*, on the other hand, is one who likes to read the familiar, who does not really want to be surprised or kept in suspense over what it is they are about to read. They might be prepared to be patient for a short time, but they do need to know immediately who the main characters in the story are going to be, what the main characters are going to be involved in and where the action is going to take place.

Iser, quoted by Stibbs (1993), neatly captures the difference between the two readers we have discussed: 'What makes a reading literary or not is the sophistication of the reader; an unsophisticated reader would find a complex novel unreadable and a sophisticated reader would find a simple novel crass'. What makes a reader sophisticated is, of course, engagement with a wide variety of reading genres, not only narrative but non-fiction as well.

Roland Barthes coined two useful terms about narrative which encapsulate something of the main difference between *Elidor* and *The Naughtiest Girl in the School*. He referred to texts as either 'lisible' (readerly) or 'scriptable' (writerly). The former are closed texts in which the writer does much of the work for the reader, filling gaps, etc., whereas the latter are much more open, the reader has to do as much work as the writer, filling gaps, inferring and creating pictures from the information given. We leave it to you to decide which is the readerly and which the writerly text!

There is a place for both kinds of narrative in the reading of our pupils. Nobody likes to be challenged constantly. At the end of a hard day, there is nothing more relaxing than to settle down with an undemanding story. On the other hand, if that is all we read, when we are faced with a narrative like *Elidor* we soon lose patience and stop reading. There were signs that many of our readers were turned off *London Fields* because that is just the kind of novel that challenges our preconceptions of what a novel is. If we are used to reading challenging novels we will probably stay with the narrative, trusting the author. If we aren't, we will give up very quickly. We must encourage our pupils, therefore, to take risks from time to time and to stay with the challenge.

We firmly believe that the reading children engage in is reflected in the development of their own narratives and the second part of this chapter is devoted to an analysis of a piece of narrative writing by a year 6 pupil.

Children's narratives

In her influential book *Children's Writing and Reading*, Katharine Perara (1984) has this to say about the written narratives of young children:

> The personal narratives which constitute such an important part of primary
> school writing typically consist of a setting, followed by a sequence of events

and a conclusion. The setting introduces the central participants and announces the timer of the action and the place where it occurs.

In terms of the setting, we can also say that most adult narratives also contain the same elements. The following story, 'Adventure Island', by Chris clearly follows the pattern suggested by Perara:

ADVENTURE ISLAND

LEVEL ONE

Chris loaded the computer. The programme 'Adventure Island' lit up the screen. He started playing. Then he got sucked into the computer. Just then he kneed the keyboard and got a cheat for infinity lives and a magic sword. Then his dog jumped in too. The dog was called Max. Chris had a weird feeling when he was in a drift tube. Then he landed. Lots of pirates came to him then, mad as anything. He started killing. He had killed them all. When he looked around all the pirates turned into coins. When he picked them up he set off. Then the dog started talking and Chris was surprised, so they started talking together. Chris decided to make a raft. They bought a shield and one each of weapons. They set off sailing. They saw a pirate ship so they speeded to it. They boarded the ship and looked in. Two skeletons came towards them. Chris got stabbed.

Max jumped on the skeleton's legs and ate them. Chris came alive again. Max ate all the bones and said, 'Very nice bones. Very nice bones'. Chris and Max looked in the cabin. There was a captain skeleton. Max said, 'Why's the skeleton in jewels? Let's find out'. Max opened his mouth and took a big bite. 'Ah', said Max. 'It is made of gold'. The ship stopped. Chris said, 'Land. Ya hoo'. A mysterious person was there. The man said, 'Hello I'm your spell caster. I will give you spells. Here is a map to show you the way'. The man disappeared. Then from the sky a voice said, 'You have completed level one. To get to the next level, defeat the enemy'.

In terms of its vocabulary, this is a fascinating piece of work. The use of terms such as 'cheat for infinity lives' and 'drift tube', which are totally meaningless to us, are evidently technical terms acquired from the new generation of computer games and support the notion that children's writing reflects their reading including, we might add, their reading of computer screens.

In terms of the sentence structure of the story, Chris uses a mixture of simple, compound and complex. There are 41 sentences, consisting of 286 words. The average sentence length is seven words; the sentences range in length from three to fourteen words.

The cohesiveness of the passage is achieved in two ways. We commented about the Blyton and Garner passages that much of their cohesiveness was obtained through pronominal usage, and the same feature is noticeable in 'Adventure Island'. The second strategy Chris uses is temporal cohesion, mainly achieved through the repetition of 'then'. The use of temporal cohesion ('then' and 'when') is very much the technique used in the stories of very young children, and suggests that Chris has not learned to vary the approach to sequencing in his writing. The story does, of course, assume a familiarity with the conventions of computer games which form its genesis. We are not sure if this is a case of intertextuality (references to other texts) or extratextuality (cultural references)! Unless you have this familiarity, the story is fairly meaningless. However, this is no more a weakness than Enid Blyton's assumption that her readers will recognize the conventions of life with a governess or being educated at a boarding school. Chris knows his audience in the same way that Enid Blyton does and is quite successful in producing an interesting and entertaining piece for that audience.

We feel that one important flaw in the writing is an overall structural weakness which results in the completion of the whole story in just over twenty lines. There is no time for the development of the characters, for example, or the details of the plot. This kind of weakness is one which occurs in thousands of young writers' work. They find it hard to know which elements to expand and which to leave alone. Perara (1984) sees this as a key component in the developing writer's ability to develop global discourse coherence in their work: 'Young writers reveal growing maturity in their control of discourse structure not only by including all the necessary components but also judging when it is appropriate to use elaborations and expansions'.

We feel that many of the sentences in 'Adventure Island' cry out for the kind of elaboration that will help readers orientate themselves much more securely in the story and begin to form a response to it which is fairly difficult to do when the whole narrative is completed so quickly. For instance, couldn't the notion of the 'weird feeling in a drift tube' be expanded considerably to add to the rather eerie atmosphere being created. There are many other sentences throughout the story that could benefit from this kind of development.

Chris's story could also be improved if there was more variation in the cohesive ties. As we discussed earlier, this is very much a 'and then . . . and then' narrative. Between a number of sentences, however, there seems to be a lack of any real cohesion and this gives the whole piece its disjointed, somewhat abrupt tone: 'The dog was called Max. Chris had a weird feeling when he was in a drift tube'. Here, as elsewhere, there is little sense of one sentence being in any way related to the previous one. New information is introduced suddenly and abruptly.

Unless a developing writer like Chris has the opportunity for discussing this kind of topic with his teacher, we feel that his writing is likely to remain at the stage indicated in 'Adventure Island': full of potential but still rather immature. One vital way for teachers to help pupils achieve this maturity is through encouraging them to read a wide variety of texts. As Margaret Meek (1983) tellingly expresses it: 'The most important single lesson that children learn from texts is the nature and variety of written discourse, the different ways that language lets a writer tell and the many and different ways a reader reads'. They not only need exposure to undemanding texts by writers with a mass popular audience, but they also need to see what else is possible even if, ultimately, they reject some genres altogether.

CHAPTER 5

Poetry: The inexhaustible ambiguity of sentences

> The reading experts, for all their understanding about 'the reading process', treat all text as the neutral substance on which the process works, as if the readers did the same thing with a poem, a timetable, a warning notice.
>
> (Meek, *How Texts Teach What Readers Learn*, 1988)

> Reading a poem is different from reading a story or any other text.
>
> (Benton and Fox, *Teaching Literature Nine to Fourteen*, 1985)

> Timothy Winters – who is he?
>
> (Response of ten-year-old to reading the poem 'Timothy Winters')

The views of Margaret Meek and Michael Benton quoted above remind us that we read a wide variety of texts every day and each makes its own demands on our reading skills. The problems posed by poems are not the same as the ones we try to grapple with in deciphering the instructions for putting together a set of kitchen furniture (sometimes poems are a lot easier to understand!) and the novel presents its own characteristic problems as we found in the last chapter.

We were interested to discover, therefore, whether the reading strategies children and adults bring to poetry are markedly different from the ones they use for narrative fiction. We tend to think that poems and novels occupy the same 'imaginative space' as each other and yet they are clearly very different in both form and function. Most obviously, poems are usually a lot shorter than novels and, as a result, far more dense in texture, much of the meaning is compressed and the kind of support and guidance provided in narrative is often missing. Indeed, to write of 'meaning' in the singular is misleading, for poems are multilayered texts.

James Thorne (1989) points out the nature of the task:

> Learning to read a poem is not a matter of learning to pay attention to the repetition of linguistic forms, phonological, lexical, or syntactic. It is a matter

of learning to hear what we must normally be deaf to: the inexhaustible ambiguity of sentences.

Such a task obviously requires of teachers that we do far more for our pupils than just teach them how to decode print. Not only must we introduce as wide a variety of reading material into the classroom as possible, but we must also teach pupils how to read each of the genres by guiding them through the characteristic features of each one.

As far as poetry is concerned, there can be few teachers, whether at primary or secondary level, for whom the words 'the poetry lesson' have not at some time in their careers caused feelings of panic and maybe anguish. Many of us must have had the experience of attempting to share with our pupils a poem for which we have the deepest feelings only to find that our pupils do not share these feelings. Indeed, they often find something comic or pathetic in the poem which we ourselves had not spotted before. The result is that we never feel the same about the poem again.

At the same time, many pupils enjoy 'writing' poetry, though their efforts sometimes fall short of the ideal as they re-work traditional poetic clichés. The following letter to the fictitious Adrian Mole from the BBC always raises a wry smile of recognition:

Dear Mr. Mole,

Thank you for submitting your last poem. I understood it perfectly well once it had been typed. However, Adrian, understanding is not all. Our Poetry Department is inundated with Autumnal poems. The smell of bonfires and the crackling of leaves pervade the very corridors . . .

Who has not gone through the ritual of finding poems about spring, summer, autumn, winter and Christmas *ad nauseam?* We use them to stimulate our pupils' imaginations in order to produce their own writing on the same theme or they provide a backdrop to the current class topic. Once we have used the same material a few times, we tend to notice a sameness about the children's response which should be a warning that it is time to do something different.

And yet poetry is something which many young children find fascinating. From early babyhood they have probably listened to nursery rhymes and experienced the enjoyment to be had from shouting out a word which sounds like one they have heard only moments before. Such responses seem also to please their parents who join in by providing new examples for the baby to try out.

Ruqaiya Hasan (1989) also points to the importance of these early experiences with nursery rhymes, by observing that infants often sway their whole bodies to the rhythms of them, thus establishing 'the foundations for the perceptions of these patterns so unobtrusively that one might be tempted to think of the ability as an innate one'. The repetition of sound in nursery rhymes also helps to develop an awareness of rhyme, alliteration and assonance because of the regularity of the repetition in nearly every example:

> Humpty Dumpty sat on a wall
> Humpty Dumpty had a great fall
> All the king's horses and all the king's men
> Couldn't put Humpty together again.

Notice, too, in 'Humpty Dumpty' the parallel structure of the two phrases in line 3 – another type of repetition. The work of Goswami and Bryant (1991) has taught us the importance of rhyme and alliteration in providing a basis for the development of phonological awareness in young children, which is so important in learning to read.

The rhymes and rhythms of nursery rhymes and poetry provide us with a sense of closure and completeness which all of us – not just children – seem to need in our lives. For many adults there is often a recognition in particular words, phrases, lines and verses that the poet has captured something fresh about a landscape, for example, so that we see it as if for the first time. Benton and Fox (1985) capture the essence of the specialness of poetry in the following comment: 'children sense immediately that there is a riddling quality to poems, something in the way words are used and laid out on the page as if the words are saying to them "we're special; we're the chosen few"'.

So when, why and how does poetry stop being fun and suddenly start to be difficult and inaccessible? Is it something to do with our own feelings of inadequacy about how to present poetry in the junior and secondary schools? Do the feelings and experiences exposed in poems demand an honesty of response from us that we are unable or unwilling to share with our pupils? Is it, as Benton (1992) claims, that 'Poetry is a problem area because many teachers either dislike it or feel ill at ease with it'. Possibly it is the specialness of poetry that puts people off. Are we perhaps as teachers afraid or reluctant to just let poetry have time to work its magic without too much assistance from us? Does it need to be 'taught' at all? Many teachers we are sure must ask questions like the following: 'I've read the poem, now what do I do with it? Do I need to ask questions and, if so, what sort?'

We were intrigued to discover how primary children and adults responded to poetry. We wondered what their responses would tell us about the way poetry is tackled in the classroom. When we worked with groups of readers on poetry, we used very much the same kind of procedure as when gathering responses to the openings of novels. We gave our readers photocopies of the poems on A4 or A3 sheets but we only photocopied one verse at a time onto a particular sheet. Our readers were asked to write down anything that occurred to them as they read the poems.

One adult reader raised serious doubts about our methodology and indeed questioned the value of any personal response to poetry at all. You might like to consider the classroom implications as you read his comments:

> I don't like this exercise. The reader goes into the poem, the object, for its own sake. What comes through the reading to the reader takes time, must evolve after absorption. The impact may be with me next week, next year, who knows? I do not want to impose my experience on the object – rather the object/poem will work through me and perhaps affect my experience.

We understand the feelings behind the first two sentences. It was T.S. Eliot, after all, who pointed out that poetry can communicate before being understood. Understanding often only comes after a period of reflection and re-reading and we would always recommend that poems are revisited in the classroom in order to provide pupils with a further opportunity to let a particular poem 'work' on them. However, we would certainly not agree with our respondent in his claim that there is no place for personal experience in the reading of poetry or any other text for that matter. It is not a question of 'imposing' experience on the text, but rather that our experience of life and other texts can often throw an illuminating light on the text that we are currently reading.

The reader we have quoted was an English graduate, and if the end result of a degree course in English is the total rejection of personal experience in the interpretation of texts, then we feel there is need for a radical rethinking of such courses.

Our adult readers formed two distinct groups. One group freely admitted that they did not read much poetry. The reticence of some readers to record their views is captured in the following comment: 'This may be a mistake. I'm not a great lover of poetry and it's not something I would actually choose to read but I'll try and be honest with my thoughts and reactions'. The same reader began to lose patience though in the middle of one poem:

> I wonder about poetry. Do people actually get paid for writing in such a pretentious way?

> My reactions to this are very difficult to judge. I understand what the message is. I just believe there are better ways of conveying it than in this form.

> Why does none of this verse rhyme?

The reader is probably expressing the views of many who never read poems in their everyday lives. She concluded her comments in the following way: 'I'm trying hard to have some kind of empathy but I'm afraid all I think of is irritation and annoyance at poetry because of the (in my opinion) disjointed way it tells its tale'.

Clearly, readers like this have never had the opportunity of just enjoying the sounds and rhythms of poetry for their own sake without feeling the need to 'explain' meaning or record comprehension in some way. For so many adults in the past and children today, the experience of poetry is filtered through the comprehension exercises in countless course books.

Our second group of adult readers was very different. They were either students training to be teachers for whom English was their chosen specialism or they were English graduates working at Dove Cottage in Grasmere, once the home of the poet William Wordsworth. For these latter readers, poetry played an important part in their lives.

We were curious to note any differences that might emerge in the reading strategies of the two groups. Both groups were given the same four poems: 'Wind' by Ted Hughes, 'Inversnaid' by Gerard Manley Hopkins, 'Overheard in County Sligo' by Gillian Clarke and 'My Aunt Dora' by Charles Causley. We selected the poems to represent a variety of styles, poets and subject matter.

At the outset we should explain that our experience of reading the responses of our readers made us question the kinds of teaching of poetry that goes on in schools and colleges/universities. At first, it was difficult to find common ground among the readers. Eventually, however, we did manage to categorize the responses under seven headings. Some readers fell exactly into one of the categories while others straddled the boundaries between one or more, although nearly all tended to show bias towards one category or another.

Adult readers

We christened one type of reader a *freewheeler*. The readers in this category tended to read very much at the level of word association, so that a word or phrase would set off a personal association which usually had nothing to do with the actual subject or theme of the poem. This, of course, also happened during the reading of the openings of the novels but, apart from the occasional reader, most readers of the novels also included other elements of response, whereas our freewheeling poetry readers tended rather to remain at the word association level. These readers seemed to finish with no real notion of what lay at the heart of a poem. One or two examples will serve to illustrate what we mean.

The phrase 'six white geese' in 'Inversnaid' produced the response, 'six geese a-laying, five gold rings', and a reference to 'force' in Ted Hughes' 'Wind' evoked, 'Darth Vadar – may the force be with you'. Such examples are perhaps very trivial and indicate readers with tongues firmly fixed in cheeks. There is no doubt that most of us respond in this type of way sometimes, particularly when we feel threatened by something we don't understand or can't deal with on an emotional or intellectual level.

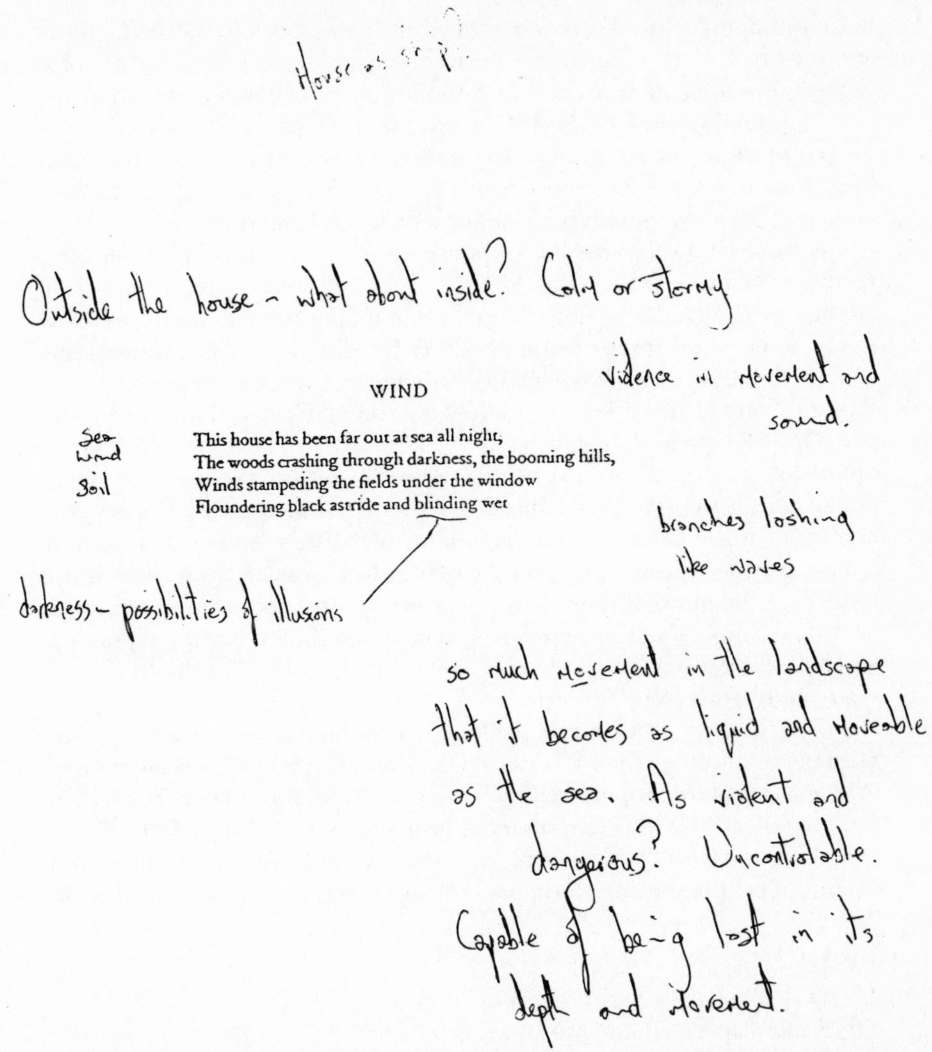

[handwritten annotation: House as s? ?]

[handwritten annotation: Outside the house - what about inside? Calm or stormy]

WIND

[handwritten annotation: Violence in movement and sound.]

[handwritten annotation: Sea wind Soil]

This house has been far out at sea all night,
The woods crashing through darkness, the booming hills,
Winds stampeding the fields under the window
Floundering black astride and blinding wet

[handwritten annotation: branches lashing like waves]

[handwritten annotation: darkness - possibilities of illusions]

[handwritten annotation: So much movement in the landscape that it becomes as liquid and moveable as the sea. As violent and dangerous? Uncontrollable. Capable of being lost in its depth and movement.]

One reader admitted incomprehension during her reading of 'Inversnaid': 'Didn't enjoy reading this as I couldn't understand half of it'. Like many of the readers of *London Fields*, such responses indicate the lack of a reading strategy strong enough to deal with 'difficult' texts.

Our second category of reader is the *lifer*. This reader made the same kind of connections between the text and their own lives as some of our novel readers. The poem 'Inversnaid' triggered a powerful memory for one reader: 'Our first sighting of wild goats as we approached Inversnaid'. Charles Causley's poem 'My Aunt Dora' produced the response: 'First World War – my father's shrapnel wound'. And the following lines from 'Overheard in County Sligo' – 'But I turn to fold the breakfast cloth and polish the lustre and the brass' – encouraged one reader to comment: 'My favourite chore at home was sitting in front of the fire with an old film on the television, polishing the brasses – especially if it was raining'. Such powerful memories evoked by a line of poetry can be a very potent means of unlocking our inner lives. Sometimes the experience is painful and forces us to confront feelings and experiences we would prefer to lie locked away undisturbed.

A somewhat different life response was apparent through such comments as: 'Rather sad – I should hate to feel like that'. Here there is an attempt by the reader to enter the emotional life of the poem in the same way as some of our novel readers tried to imagine themselves in the same sort of situation as a character in the narrative. In the response above, though, there is an evident desire to keep the experience at arm's length.

The two types of reader we have observed so far belong very firmly on the left-hand side of our reading model, the personal response side (see p. 51). This is the side we firmly believe should be given more status in the classroom as the basis for encouraging further discussion of poems. There is a danger that we only focus on the text without investigating what brings it to life in the mind of the reader. However, on their own, these somewhat unstructured personal responses are inadequate in helping the reader get a rich reading of the text and, as we have already noticed in the freewheeling readers, sometimes ignore it altogether.

The category of reader we decided to call the *translator* could not have been more different than the freewheeler and the lifer. Translators failed to take any account of personal responses at all and focused entirely on the text, seeing it as a foreign language which had to be transformed into acceptable English. Verses were rewritten, paraphrased or summarized. The wonderfully evocative language of the second verse of Ted Hughes' 'Wind':

. . . then under an orange sky
The hills had new places, and wind wielded
Blade – light, luminous black and emerald,
Flexing like the lens of a mad eye,

encouraged one reader to observe, 'Day break brought a change in the weather – wind still strong'. And from the poem 'Inversnaid', the line 'But I turn to fold the breakfast cloth' is summarized by another reader as, 'Realisation that she is stuck with her lot'. This type of reading seems to view the poem as a comprehension exercise there to be reshaped or rephrased to indicate that understanding has been achieved and no doubt reflects some readers' experience of poetry lessons at school.

Many of our readers who were English graduates had obviously been taught to respond to poetry in particular ways and because of this we refer to them simply as *trained* readers. One such reader noted: 'This is a good poem. And I'm aware that I read as a trained reader – that my thoughts are in/on the poem – I cut out the extraneous before the object'.

We subdivided these readers into two subcategories. One type of reader we decided to call the *texter*. This reader focused on how the poem 'worked'. Typical of the comments under this category were: 'Language highlights the fact of the poem – I like 'flutes' – breaks the roll of the verse'. The trained texter was also likely to make intertextual allusions: 'The tarot makes me think of T.S. Eliot (Madam Sosostris in 'The Waste Land'). However, in this particular case, the intertextual reference did not appear to help the reader gain any real insight into the poem because the connection between the reader's response and the poet's intention was tenuous at best. Like many freewheeling responses, such links *can* be rewarding but are often just random associations between reader and text.

Our second category of trained reader we call the *technique spotter*. This reader simply picked out poetic devices and noted them with such comments as: 'vivid use of metaphor'. This seemed an arid exercise in the main, with most readers failing to go beyond the simple recognition of the particular device and with no attempt to show how it worked in the appropriate context. Moreover, an adjective such as 'vivid' does not really convey any meaning. It is the sort of vague term which often passes for literary criticism in the book reviews of newspapers.

The following comment in which the reader seems to have in his grasp all the vocabulary necessary for literary analysis is typical of the approach which sees the spotting of poetic devices as more important than honest response. Alongside verse I of Hopkins' 'Inversnaid' the reader had noted: 'Hopkins' sprung rhythm intense language constant use of alliteration very deliberate language'.

Reproduced below is the complete response by one reader to the Gillian Clarke poem and we would ask whether these kinds of comment actually tell us anything about the feelings or experiences captured in the poem? Do they help the reader's understanding of what lies at the heart of it?

Narrative
Lyrical – 'painterly'
Single point – seriousness wrapped in commonplace
1st person
Single pov [point of view]
Everyday language
Limited opportunity
Dreams are beyond social etc. conditions
Social realism

Surely this kind of analysis is pointless unless the reader can actually point to the precise effect of the techniques being used in terms of the poem as a whole. One of our readers in fact commented rather bitterly about the sort of 'A' level training which exploits this way of approaching literary texts:

> Some people will probably write something deep and meaningful about the choice of words or length of lines or something but that's only 'cos they think that's what you want to hear! When you've analysed 100's of poems you think you immediately have to look at alliteration, choice of words etc.

This seems to be a fairly damning indictment of the traditional approach to poems at 'A' level and beyond, and certainly many students we have taught appear to believe that poetry analysis means technique spotting to the exclusion of everything else, including personal response.

Other readers in this category commented on the imagery of poems. One pleasing difference between comments on images and those on other poetic devices was that at least comments about the images were usually accompanied by statements about the effect of the image on the reader: 'Superb image – I can see a tent floundering in a storm, with pegs and ropes lashing about'. This comment was made during a reading of 'Wind'. Other readers actually drew pictures to reinforce the visual response evoked by some images.

Other responses indicated readers attempting to articulate the effects of various aspects of poems on their feelings or emotions but often lacking the vocabulary to do so. Such readers fell back to using empty adjectives like 'super', 'perfect', 'vivid' or 'good'. This is not necessarily intended as criticism of such responses. One of the powerful reasons for reading poetry is that a poem can often verbalize experience and emotion in a way we ourselves have never been able to articulate. One reader also caught well the dilemma that poetry sometimes poses: 'should I read it fast and enjoy the words – or try and sort it out?' Many teachers will recognize this kind of response and sympathize with it, we are sure. It's something that crops up almost every time we use poetry with our pupils. How much do we need to 'explain' and how much do we just leave to the sheer magic of the poem itself?

Finally, we did find one reader who responded at a personal level but then tried to examine how the poem was working in order to affect her in such ways. Equal weight was given both to the part played by the reader and the demands of the text. We gave this reader the category title *complete reader* not because her responses were totally 'complete' (there is no such completeness, as our chapter heading indicates), but rather because they reflected both sides of the reading model. A comment on Gillian Clarke's 'Overheard in County Sligo' exemplifies her approach:

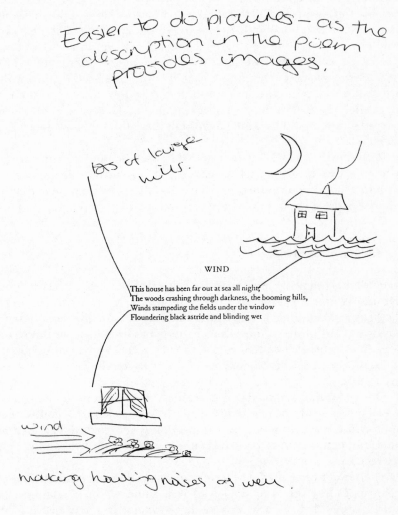

Easier to do pictures — as the description in the poem provides images.

lots of large hills.

WIND

This house has been far out at sea all night,
The woods crashing through darkness, the booming hills,
Winds stampeding the fields under the window
Floundering black astride and blinding wet

wind

making howling noises as well.

A very empty desolate life . . . this all seems reflected by the repetitive rhyme and rhythm of the poem. No sense of hope or change. Very simple rhyme scheme and the poem ends where it started as if it will be repeated again and again. Her life will never change.

In these comments we feel that the reader has successfully combined her feelings evoked by the poem with an ability to stand back and point out the technical means by which the poet has aroused those feelings.

Before we go on to discuss the responses of children to poetry, we would like to summarize briefly our findings from the adult readers. We found very few readers engaging in what Michael Benton (1992) has called 'a series of literary "double-takes"' during the reading of a poem. By this Benton meant that reading poetry involves a constant interaction between our interpretation of the words at one level and, at a second level, our own personal responses to the words, after reflection and consideration. Most of our readers seemed to be engaged at either one level or the other, with a third group seeing the text as a sort of literary puzzle where the aim is to spot the devices used by the poet to conceal the real meaning of the poem. Few readers attempted the kind of synthesis that our *complete reader* was able to achieve.

With this in mind, together with Michael Benton's comment that poetry 'needs to be given back to readers', we now turn to the question of how primary children respond to poetry. Did the same kinds of issues that we have discussed in the adults' responses crop up?

Children's responses

We used the following poems with our primary readers: 'Hairy Toe', 'Timothy Winters', 'Eddie and the Shreddies', 'Alone in the Grange', 'The Frozen Man' and 'a heavy rap'. We gave exactly the same instructions as we had given to our adult readers, basically to write down anything that occurred to them as they read the individual verses of the poems. All the pupils we worked with were between the ages of nine and eleven years.

One point that emerged very quickly when we began to read through the comments made by children was that it was possible to analyse their responses according to the same classification system that we had used for adults although, as might be expected, there were no readers who came into the trained reader category.

There were certainly freewheelers among the young readers. The example opposite gives a good idea of how some of the readers in this category responded. Clearly, this reader is totally at a loss as to how to respond to the poem. All the responses from this child were similarly random and uncoordinated. It is clear that, for pupils like this, poetry has lost its power to inspire in any way at all. How can we deal with pupils for whom poetry has been such a negative or non-existent experience?

Brian Merrick (1993) sees it as a matter of selection of appropriate material for our pupils and, following selection: 'What to do with them in the classroom then centres on the question of how to present the poem in a way or in circumstances that may release the life – the magic in the stone'.

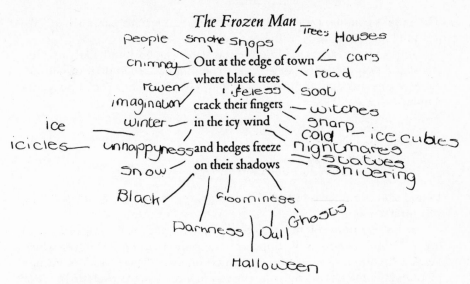

The rather sad example of 'The Frozen Man' we quoted above indicates how little of the magic of poetry rubs off on to many children as a result of their classroom experiences. We discuss this issue in greater detail in the final chapter of the book: 'Implications for the Classroom'.

As well as examples of freewheeling responses, we also found some readers who we could relate to the lifer category, with the following example fairly typical of a response to an action performed by somebody in one of the poems: 'I would not do that'. We find it fascinating that children should make this matter-of-fact kind of comment. It seems to show that already there is the demand that poetry reflects everyday life, and a reluctance to take on its own level the magic, fantasy and sometimes otherworldliness that poetry offers.

One reader, responding to the poem 'a heavy rap', indicated a very sceptical point of view. The verse:

> i had a jumping contest with a kangaroo and jumped clear outa australia and
> passed the astronauts
> on their way back down

was accompanied by the single word: 'bull'! Another reader used the following lines from 'Eddie and the Shreddies':

> sometimes he forgets where his mouth is and stuffs a Shreddie in his ear,

to comment: 'you never forget where your mouth is'. And a lovely comment was made by one pupil in response to the following line in 'Timothy Winters':

> eyes as wide as a football pool.

The pupil's comment was: 'If he's like that what are his parents like?' We can only speculate, along with our reader!

One or two readers fell into the translator category and, like our adult translators, saw the text as something to be summarized in their own terms. At various points during the opening stanza of 'The Hairy Toe', one reader wrote:

> stops singing and starts screaming,
> wakes up suddenly
> jumps back into bed
> a trembling lump under the covers

In addition, there were a few observations on the quality of texts: 'Not a very interesting line'.

However, none of the children could be classified as texters. Two other distinct categories did appear in the responses of the children which merit a mention. One group we termed imagers. These readers formed pictures and images very much in the way that readers of novels do in order to fill gaps and obtain a consistent reading of the text. Our readers made comments like: 'I can see an old woman walking in a gale with the hairy toe'. One reader chose to respond to each verse of 'Alone in the Grange' by writing a series of responses each beginning: 'I can see . . .'. Other children chose to draw the pictures they visualized around the text of the poem. Imaging is recognized as something many readers do in response to a novel or poem and, although some of our adults did respond in this powerful way, we were surprised that more of them did not.

We use the label questioner for our final group of readers. They asked questions of the text, not in the same way as our readers asked questions of the novel openings in an endeavour to find out what might be coming next, but really to express uncertainty as to the meaning of what they had read, as if they had not been given enough information to form a consistent reading of the particular poem. In Charles Causley's 'Timothy Winters', the opening line provoked such questions as: 'Who is he?', 'What school?' This uncertainty is also brought sharply into focus by one pupil who did not understand the line: 'Through his britches the blue winds blow'. The pupil queried this line: 'Blue wind? But you can't see the wind'. It appeared to us that some of our readers could not accept the fact that poetry often calls for a leap of the imagination in an effort to make connections between our own experience (of life, relationships, the way things are, language and so on) and that offered by the poem.

Our adult readers did not raise questions about the poetry in the same way as the pupils. Either, we feel, because of their greater knowledge of what poetry is like or, perhaps, they had lots of questions to ask but did not want to admit this. In fact, only a very small number of adults raised questions in the same tentative, hesitant way that many of our young readers did. It may, for example, have accounted for the translators. An easy way out of a problem is to put down everything you *do* know. A technique many of us have used in examination contexts!

The issues we have raised in the discussion are obviously many and varied. There was a tremendous variety in the range of responses we received, though many of them were the result of random and uncoordinated readings. Overall, we were left with the feeling that poetry is a 'problem' for many readers. The challenge for the teacher is what to do about that challenge. One response might be to avoid poetry altogether, although the National Curriculum requirements make this strategy impossible. Moreover, there are other deeper reasons for persevering with poetry in the classroom. As Benton (1992) points out: 'To deprive children of poems is to deny them the society of clear, single voices and an irreplaceable range of feeling. We neglect poetry at our peril.'

In the final chapter of the book, we will return to the presentation of poetry in the classroom in order to clarify the main approaches which we believe can help many of our pupils to feel more comfortable in the presence of the voices and feelings to be found there.

CHAPTER 6

Advertising: Legal, decent, honest and truthful?

They [pupils] should be shown how to distinguish between fact and opinion in a variety of texts, including newspapers, magazines and advertisements.
(National Curriculum Programmes of Study for EN2)

A London conference of advertising and marketing executives yesterday wrestled with a report on what they called 'kidese' (slang language) in an effort to sell more effectively to young people.
(*Daily Telegraph*, 22 August 1992)

The M and Ms advert is good because I love M and Ms.
(Ten-year-old after watching a series of TV advertisements)

Our quote from the current (1994) National Curriculum document serves to remind us that we referred in Chapter 1 to the proposed changes to the current English curriculum published in April 1993, whereby the requirement to use media texts at Key Stage Two had been removed. At the time of writing this chapter, it seems that wiser counsels have prevailed, as we understand that such a change is not to be implemented.

The past few years have, in fact, seen many teachers beginning to introduce media texts into the English curriculum, not only because they play an important part in the lives of young children and, as such, are something children are interested in, but because they are also a source of useful material for analysis in the classroom. We firmly believe that newspapers and adverts, for example, should take their place as texts worthy of discussion and analysis.

We can use discussion about such texts in order to demonstrate how the language and pictures are often used to manipulate opinion or to persuade us to buy products. Advertisers present an image of the world which raises hopes and expectations that merely buying a particular product is enough to improve our appearance or lifestyle to match the one presented in the advert. The trouble is that every advertiser is playing the same game, so that no sooner have we bought one product guaranteed to make our lives complete than we realize we need something else being marketed by another company. And so it goes on and on and on. As Gary Day (1990) notes: 'Advertising promotes insecurity. It encourages consumers to believe in a state of affairs – Utopia or their own perfectability – which can never be realised'.

All this may seem a long way from the material of the previous three chapters of the book. But we were keen to gauge responses to a variety of genres. Most of us come into contact with adverts almost every day of our lives in some form or other and we were interested to compare the responses of children and adults to adverts with the responses we had obtained for novels and poems.

On the face of it, adverts and poems are at opposite ends of the literary spectrum. Or are they? In one way we can think of both as linked to the notion of persuasion. Obviously, the advertiser wants us to buy a particular product and does so by trying to convince us that we need it to make a change in order to enhance our lives. The poet, too, is trying to persuade us to change by engaging our sensibilities in order to change our perceptions of some aspect of the world in which we live. It is maybe not surprising, then, that many of the techniques used in advertisements are also the stock-in-trade of the poet.

The techniques shared by poets and advertisers, such as rhyme, alliteration, syntactic and typographical patterning, puns, images and so on, are all meant to catch our eyes and ears and engage our interest in order to bring about changes in our behaviour patterns. The effect of a good poem is, of course, rather different from the observable changes produced by a successful advert; nevertheless, a powerful poem does change us.

We wanted to find out how far adults and children were aware of some of the techniques used by advertisers and whether they could articulate how and why the techniques were being used. In addition, we were curious to discover whether advertising texts were 'read' in the same ways as literary texts. For our adult readers we selected four adverts from a variety of sources: *Radio Times*, a weekend colour supplement, a woman's weekly magazine and one from the new generation of magazines aimed at the affluent male. The adults were given exactly the same instructions as for the poems. What was fascinating about their responses was that it proved possible to categorize them in exactly the same way as for the poetry responses with the addition of one new category. A selection of comments is given below under the appropriate categories.

The sun's shining, the hood's down and you have a journey to make. Any driver would relish the prospect; the driver of a Lotus Elan will enjoy a special treat.

The Elan, after all, has a chassis and suspension which set it apart. Our patented 'raft' front suspension endows the Elan with great cornering potential, yet also delivers the highest levels of ride compliance and feel. Add the 165bhp turbocharged engine and the cocktail is complete. A package which is showing the world how a modern sports car should be: fast, stable fuel efficient, brilliantly packaged, timeless lines. A Lotus.

For a test drive with your nearest dealer or for a brochure, call Lotusline on 071-253 7073 (24 hours).

Don't like the original poem — hated doing it at 'A' level- would turn over in disgust!

Why is he in a car instead of climbing those beautiful hills — if you want to joy ride - try the M1!

White/ young (ish) man in a sports car — not very Cocktail! — reinforcing white upper middle class subtle. imagery.

Patronising text.

Trying to impress with jargon that doesn't necessarily mean anything ie "raft"

Freewheeler

The sort of unfocused response apparent in some of the responses to poems also cropped up in the comments about adverts. Thus, the word 'licence' in one advert encouraged the contextually irrelevant response 'car' in one reader. One reader, noting the use of a trademark symbol after the name of a product, proudly claimed: 'I can do these on my PC now'.

Of more interest were some of the responses which an advert for Lotus cars stimulated. The Lotus logo which encloses the name of the company brought out the following comments: 'speed', 'Dream car ££££s', and the following was one reader's reaction to the complete advert which contained a colour photograph of a young man driving among lakes and mountains: 'That's me in 5 years driving round Windermere'. The banner heading in the Lotus advert – 'Far From the Madding Crowd' – seemed to hint at literary snobbery for one reader: 'Why is it OK for Hardy?'

We were in fact surprised that there were not more responses on the word association level. Some advertisers spend years creating an image for a company so that the mere mention of the name is enough to set off particular associations. How do you react to the words 'Chanel' or 'Georgio Armani'? It is difficult to prevent such words from triggering off particular associations. In this sense, of course, they are not freewheeling responses because the associations are carefully controlled by the advertiser. Sometimes, though, it can go wrong for the company. What associations does the word 'Skoda' conjure up?

Lifer

As discussed in the previous chapter, a 'lifer' is someone who sees in a text a direct link with their own life experience. The distinction between freewheeling responses and lifer responses can be a bit difficult to sustain, particularly if, on occasion, we really mean to achieve the kind of perfectability promised by a product. Many readers did in fact make connections between what they had seen in adverts and their own life experience. One of our adverts was for the Halifax Building Society. The opening sentence in the main text read: 'When your kids leave home why not live a little'. One reader wrote: 'My parents are "doing". They're never in when I 'phone'. Another reader pointed out something important about our motivation for reading some adverts in greater detail than normal. In reading the building society advert, she wrote: 'I'd read this now as I'm interested in mortgages. Wouldn't have a year ago'.

The invitation to ring a 'phone number for a test drive of a Lotus car plainly raised feelings of dissatisfaction with her age and appearance for one reader: 'If I thought I looked older and responsible (and rich) I'd have 'phoned them straightaway to get a test drive'. One reader entered a note of scepticism about a claim in an advert for a slimming product that up to 4lb could be lost in a week by writing: 'Not necessary to do this to lose 4lb. I'm bringing prior knowledge to this'.

Translator

Few of our readers felt the need to paraphrase sections of texts in adverts. We only found one example. Presumably most readers find such texts relatively straightforward with no need for translation. Interestingly, the one piece of translation we found related to an advertisement for the Post Office. This was in the form of a rather sentimental narrative and stimulated many readers to scorn or sympathy. One reader translated one section with the sentence: 'He's laughing with his friends, she's sitting knitting with her friends'.

Texter/technique spotter

It was difficult to distinguish between these two categories as far as the responses to adverts were concerned, so we have included both under the single phrase 'technique spotter'. Some readers did make intertextual allusions to other texts, such as 'Postman Pat' (responding to the village green illustration used in a Post Office advert), but most tended to focus on recognizing technical devices used by the advertiser. The Lotus advert which contained some language needing a specialist knowledge produced the following: 'Trying to impress with jargon that doesn't necessarily mean anything'. The lengthy double-page advert for the Post Office did not impress some of our readers. One response was: 'No punchy lines – not a good advert, very unclear'. A major difference between these responses and the ones we discussed in the last chapter lies in the confidence of the readers of adverts to make firm judgements about the effectiveness of a technique (or, as in the last example quoted, lack of it).

One reader noted 'a narrative' about the Post Office advert and another spotted an example of onomatopoeia in another, but these were unusual. We thought one reader was on the point of raising an important issue by underlining the word 'our' in a Theakston's advert and asking the question: 'Who is our?' Unfortunately, the reader took this no further. But this technique is one method advertisers employ to imply a relationship with the reader or viewer. It suggests a world of shared interests and values and it does not take long to find examples of other adverts in which pronouns such as 'we' and 'us' proliferate. Such a practice suggests a bond which is spurious or synthetic. This is the kind of technique we do well to resist as individuals.

In summary, most of the comments were to be found under the lifer category. But there were quite a number of comments that could be grouped together into a category which had no parallel in the poetry responses. In several of the adverts, our readers challenged statements and claims made by the advertiser. This applied in particular to statements in an advert for Carnation Slender. The following example indicates the bluntness of some of the responses. The claim 'Be up to 4lbs lighter a week from today', received the comment 'lies' from one reader. One reader had ringed the word 'kid' in the Halifax Building Society example and objected to its usage and also the theme of the advert: 'I don't like this language or central theme'. Similarly, some readers felt able to pass judgements about the whole message in some adverts: 'sick', 'eyewash' and 'Aah! How sweet', were some of the comments recorded. We would characterize such comments as *personal judgement* and distinguish them from the comments made by the trained reader by emphasizing that the personal judgements were made from the perspective of the reader, whereas the trained readers' comments were more text-referenced.

The comments under the personal judgement category fulfilled the same function as the equally strong judgements passed by our readers about whether they would carry on reading past the first page of the novels. The readers of the adverts are in effect saying that they reject (or accept) the message of the advert and would not (or would) buy the product, just as their judgements about novels indicated an acceptance or rejection of the message being offered there.

It is interesting that nearly all our readers who passed such judgements about adverts rejected the claims they had read. It seems that we go to novels or poems wanting to be drawn in, whereas we want to resist the blandishments of the advertiser. If our readers are typical of the population at large, we might ask: 'Why do advertisers bother?' This is possibly a case of rhetoric not being confirmed by reality; our *actual* behaviour being at odds with what we think we *should* do.

It was very noticeable that there were far fewer comments on the advertisements than on either novels or poems. This may have been due to several factors. Our readers may well not have been used to reading adverts very closely. They are so much part of the furniture of everyday life that they can slip into our minds without our really noticing, and the idea of responding to such familiar material may have seemed strange to some readers.

In addition, most of our adults had probably never been given a framework within which to analyse such texts, either at school or later. With novels and poems most people know the agenda even if only vaguely. How do we read adverts? What kind of language is appropriate to such a task?

Children's responses

One of the rules in the British Code of Advertising Practice reads as follows:

> No advertisement should cause children to believe that they will be inferior to other children, or unpopular with them, if they do not buy a particular product, or have it bought for them.

On the face of it, this self-imposed regulation on the advertising industry appears to offer protection to children from the potential excesses of some advertisers. The words 'on the face of it' are important because what the regulation does not do is to protect children from being drawn into the role of consumer, a role that enables advertisers to target them specifically, even to the extent of using the appropriate slang or colloquialisms, as the report from a conference of advertising executives indicated at the head of this chapter. Once we have assumed the consumer role, it is very difficult to stand back from it in order to take a more objective view and ask questions like: 'Do I really need this product?'

Haven't we all seen over the past few years the kind of pressure that children can bring to bear on parents to persuade them to buy products associated with Ninja Turtles or Jurassic Park. Books, films and a variety of merchandise are often accompanied by expensive advertising campaigns aimed at children. The result is a short-lived but often obsessive interest by many children which can have knock-on effects in school. How many teachers, we wonder, have had to ban children from writing any more stories about turtles or dinosaurs?

It is difficult to gauge the long-term effect on individual children of such campaigns. As Carol Craggs (1992) points out: 'Although much has been written about children's comprehension of adverts, generally it is unwise to make assumptions about what is really understood'. What is certainly true is that they are learning to be consumers living in a world where it appears to be essential to buy what everybody else is buying.

We wanted to discover whether children had the same kind of sceptical approach to adverts that many of our adults displayed. We did realize, however, that they would have even less of a conceptual framework within which to discuss adverts than our adult respondents. With this in mind, we used a somewhat different approach to the advertising texts when working with a group of year 6 pupils in a small school in Cumbria.

Initially, we played them a videotape of a number of adverts chosen at random. The tape contained about ten minutes of adverts. We followed this up with a group discussion and then asked the pupils to choose one of the adverts to write about. Later, we gave the group four printed adverts for products which we thought would be of interest to them and we asked them to record their initial impressions of each example and then to look at the adverts more closely and write about anything else that caught their attention as they read on.

Watching the videotape with the pupils proved an absorbing experience. Their reactions to individual adverts demonstrated how powerful and successful this type of persuasion is. The children laughed at the antics of 'characters' involved in the adverts, recited whole chunks of discourse in unison from adverts they were familiar with, and joined in the chorus from the Ford advert: 'Everything we do is driven by you'. They might have been watching well-loved films, sitcoms or soaps or listening to popular records. Indeed, they wanted us to play more recordings after break and were disappointed that we hadn't got any more to offer them!

We asked the children to choose a favourite from the ones we had shown them and they found no difficulty in doing so. Their comments indicate a mixture of naïvety and sophistication in that there was both a sense of enjoyment in some of the situations created on TV commercials and a knowingness about the kinds of free gifts or special offers often featured on national advertising campaigns. This ambivalence is apparent in Angela's remark about an advert for Persil:

> I think the Persil advert is good because it has a rhyme when it says a spring clean and I like it when the lady and the little girl is hanging the washing out. With some adverts they get you to buy it by putting a prize on it or go on a holiday. At the moment on the Quavers packet there is a computer and inside the packet there is a red square and it will tell you if you have won or lost.

Several of the oral and written responses from pupils could be classed within our lifer category, as indicated by the following: 'I know they're good trainers because lots of people buy them and they're trendy too'. When one pupil read an advert that appeared to be for the Steven Spielberg film *Hook*, he quickly realized that the advert was not for the film itself but for some associated merchandise: 'I spotted the name Ocean because it's the name of software'.

Of particular interest during the discussion were the comments about an advertisement for Pepsi which featured Michael Jackson. The children were full of stories about the supposed disfigurement to Michael Jackson's face as a result of plastic surgery (the discussion took place some time before more unsavoury stories began to appear in the press and on television). Such stories seemed to add to his mystique. Like the freewheeling comments from adults, the pupils' remarks indicated the success of the advertiser in removing the reader/viewer from the here-and-now to a fantasy world through the use of verbal and visual images.

However, one pupil wrote later that the offer made on the Pepsi advert for free tickets to a Michael Jackson concert was not all it might seem:

> I like the Michael Jackson advert because it had Michael Jackson in it. But the advert when it was about Pepsi was a bit of a bribe. It was a bribe because if you liked Michael Jackson you would want to go and see him in a concert. And by going to see him you would have to buy a Pepsi can because you could win something to see him.

We think we follow the argument! From the discussion it was clear that the young lady who wrote the above knew that advertisers do not offer something for nothing.

Many of the pupils in the group had similar confidence in refuting the claims of advertisers as our adult readers in the personal judgement category. One boy was puzzled by a photograph in an advert for mountain bikes. The photo showed someone on a bike coming down a steep, rocky mountain. The comment that followed was: 'I don't know how that boy can ride down a mountain on a bike. You would think a lighter bike would be a lot weaker but it says on the advert it is stronger'. A further example illustrates personal judgement being supported by life experience:

> The M and M advert is good because I love M and Ms. The bit what says the milk chocolate melts in your hand isn't true. I put lots of M and Ms in my hand and held them for a while and whatever colour the M and M was that colour was all over my hand.

Apart from a general ability to demonstrate a healthy unwillingness to suspend belief, none of the children we worked with really knew anything about the techniques used by advertisers to put across their messages. Most of the children did realize that you do not get something for nothing in life and this enabled them to see through some of the enticements on offer. This would, we feel, offer a basis for further work in the classroom on this topic. As Carol Craggs (1992) notes:

> Clearly young people are not totally duped by everything they see in commercials, but they do watch and enjoy them and presumably buy, or put pressure on their parents to buy some of the merchandise.

One way into the study of adverts might be to look at some of the verbs frequently used to order or command us to do something: 'buy', 'get', 'use' are obvious examples. Once children pick up the idea they can profitably use it to create their own commercials, either on video or in the form of posters for specific products.

The vocabulary or register used for particular types of products is another useful area. What are the typical words and phrases used by beauty product companies or estate agents? Once a group has examined some examples and collected a list of words such as 'natural', 'environmentally friendly' and other words often used in the world of beauty products, some work could be done in defining just what these terms mean. It soon becomes clear that many of them are meaningless bits of jargon and such a demonstration throws into sharp relief the emptiness of many of the claims made for such goods.

Carol Craggs (1992), whose excellent book on using the mass media in the primary classroom we have quoted several times, has some sensible advice on the general principles to be adopted in starting out on any work related to advertising:

> Learning about advertising must be in response to the children's own experiences, pleasures and understanding, and the teaching must take its direction from what the pupils already know and what they need to understand about commercials in order to enable them to develop their critical faculties.

Such development is at the heart of why we feel it is important for teachers to use adverts in junior classrooms. If we can help children towards an objective appraisal of advertising texts, we will have given them a tool for analysing language which they can also use in other areas of life where language is used to persuade and mislead.

In approaching poetry in the classroom, we feel teachers should encourage personal response at the expense of textual analysis. What we are recommending in the study of advertising texts runs counter to this. While showing that adverts are skilfully made and can be enjoyable to watch and read, we should also be emphasizing the right-hand side of our reading mode (see p. 51) in pointing to the techniques involved in putting together such texts.

We have suggested one or two starting points for this work. These starting points can lead to further challenging work in which children are given the opportunities to create their own media texts using the same techniques as the professionals. We empower our pupils in working in this way to 'see through' language. That is, we help them to use language as a creative and imaginative tool. But we are also helping them to see through the ideology of language by showing that language can be used to manipulate or persuade us against our will to a particular behaviour pattern.

The discussion about poetry in the last chapter and advertising in the current one have added extra dimensions to the model of reading we provided at the end of Chapter 3. The freewheeling, lifer and personal judgement responses that have emerged from the discussion of poems and adverts clearly belong to the left-hand side of our model, that concerned with the reader. The translator, texter and technique spotter are responses arising from the linguistic or generic challenges of the text and, as such, fit into the right-hand side of the model.

We feel that one of the main implications of the model for teachers in the primary classroom is the need to weigh the demands of particular types of text against the importance of encouraging and stimulating personal response in pupils. It is essential that both sides of the model are given appropriate emphasis according to the nature of the text being used at any one time. In the following chapter, we look in more detail at the classroom implications of the discussion that has developed in Chapters 3, 4 and 5.

CHAPTER 7

Implications for the classroom

To foster in pupils a love of literature, to encourage their awareness of its unique relationship to human experience and to promote in them a sense of excitement in the power and potential of language can be one of the greatest joys of the English teacher. It is also one of the greatest challenges.

Media education . . . deals with fundamental aspects of language, interpretation and meaning.

(*English for Ages 5 to 16* – Proposals for the Secretary of State, June 1989)

In 1988, Brian Cox was asked to chair the committee which was to produce the National Curriculum for English, and in his book *Cox on Cox* (1992) he traces the history of that committee, the documents it produced and their reception by government ministers. The above quotation is taken from the original set of proposals which was made up of three sections: an underlying rationale, programmes of study and attainment targets. However, when the proposals were finalized in the 'yellow ring binder', the underlying rationale had disappeared. Only the programmes of study and attainment levels were printed. The result was a national curriculum aimed at developing children as speakers, listeners, readers and writers which appeared to have no rationale underpinning it. (There was further ministerial insistence that the attainment targets preceded the programmes of study – the reasons for which we can only guess.) One aim of *Cox on Cox* was to make available the original rationale and the whole of the second half of the book is a reprint of it. Cox argues for teachers needing an understanding of why they are covering particular areas with children and why they are assessing children in particular aspects of their work.

Because the rationale had 'disappeared', the focus of this book, response to literature, became an area in the National Curriculum with no explanation attached to it, and in Chapter 1 we examined the use of the word 'response' in the statutory orders and the first re-write. The two sides to response, the part played by the reader and the demands of the text, are not clearly defined, so that in our experience many primary teachers are unaware of quite what is involved. This is despite a great deal of work over the last ten years or so in which it has been argued that reader-response represents an exciting approach to literature with children (for example, Protherough 1983; Benton and Fox 1985; Chambers 1985; Hunt 1991). The aim of this book is to demonstrate what this looks like when we examine the response of very young children, primary age children and adults, looking for connections and seeing what development might look like. Wherever the word 'response' occurs in the reading attainment targets and programme of study, the aspects of reading on which we have focused are directly relevant.

The previous chapters have been concerned with readers responding to literary texts and advertisements and we have moved from pre-school children sharing picture books at home with their parents, through children in the primary classroom to adults. We have suggested that many aspects of the process remain the same, not least the ways in which readers make connections between their own lives and the fictional texts they read (or have read to them). As we 'develop' as readers, we are able to meet the demands of an increasing range of texts in which a variety of techniques may be employed. We are also able to stand back from texts and appreciate the ways in which they work – important in literary texts but vital with regard to the media. The need to 'resist' the text, not allowing it to work on us, has major implications if the aim of the text is to make us think in certain ways (or to spend our money on particular items). Indeed, the ideologies which lie behind both literary and media texts, especially if they are implicitly assumed and so not necessarily obvious to the reader, need recognizing by anyone using any text in the classroom. However, while underlying textual ideologies have not traditionally been a focus for teachers, the text most certainly has been. Extracting the supposed 'meaning' of texts has been the major aim of class work (usually under the banner of 'comprehension'). It is the reader side of the reading equation which has been neglected. Yet how we read will depend on a variety of factors both in the text and ourselves [the quotation from A.S. Byatt's (1990) *Possession* at the head of Chapter 1 summarizes this superbly]. We do not always respond to literature in the same way. In Chapter 4, we found one clear example of a reader who not only described the ways in which the poems affected her, but was also able to recognize the techniques employed by the poets which enabled the poems to have those effects. For her, reading literature was obviously a powerful experience and not just an analysis of techniques. The analysis becomes fascinating in order to examine how literature comes to induce the responses which it does. If such reading is the aim, we need to ask how this will look in the primary classroom. What is important in the development of children as readers and writers? Which aspects of the process have implications for the ways in which we use stories, novels, rhymes and poetry with children? How might we approach advertisements? We examine the implications in three sections, beginning with the experiences of children in the pre-school years, moving on to the early years of schooling and then considering reading with older primary children.

From home to school

What does the child know?

Chapter 2 examines response to literature in the early years and the first implication for the teacher is to determine just what a child has learnt during the pre-school years. Just as response has two 'sides', a reader and a text, so we need to consider a child's learning in terms of what reading means to the child as well as what has been learnt about texts and how they work.

The reader

In terms of the child (the 'reader'), perhaps the most important factor will be the view the child has of reading. In *Ways with Words*, Shirley Bryce Heath (1983) gives a fascinating account of the attitudes towards literacy of three different communities in the United States: 'Trackton', a black, working-class community; 'Roadville', a white, working-class community; and 'Townspeople', a white, middle-class community. The ways in which reading and writing were viewed and used varied in the communities, but in each case the most common was the *instrumental*: 'Reading to gain information for meeting practical needs of daily life' (e.g. price tags, labels, reminder notes). Another important use was *news-related*: 'Reading to gain information about third parties or distant events' (e.g. newspapers). Literature as a 'use' of reading does not figure at all in Trackton, while in Roadville it is only mentioned as 'bedtime stories for pre-schoolers' under the heading *recreational/educational*, the least occurring use. For the Townspeople, reading 'popular novels' occurs as part of *critical/educational*, the fourth out of six uses.

These different cultural views of literacy are a challenge to all teachers in the early years – the home visits in England described by Hilary Minns (1990) in *Read It To Me Now* make the same point. Certainly, literature is seen to have very low prestige in two of the communities, with popular novels only appearing as part of the Townspeople's reading. Only in Roadville are children's bedtime stories mentioned. Children growing up in any of the homes in these communities will not necessarily arrive at school with a view of reading as a powerful 'literary' experience. They will have different ideas of what reading means, centred on its use for different purposes. Most teachers see the development of a love of reading for its own sake as a major aim of their work and indeed we would include ourselves in this. However, the following quotation from *Ways with Words* (also quoted by Minns) makes us aware of the complexities involved:

> Reading was a public group affair for almost all members of Trackton from the youngest to the oldest. Miss Lula sometimes read her bible alone, and Annie May would sometimes quietly read magazines she brought home, but to read alone was frowned upon, and individuals who did so were accused of being anti-social. Aunt Berta had a son who as a child used to slip away from the cotton field and read under a tree. He is now a grown man with children, and has obtained a college degree, but the community still tells tales about his peculiar boyhood habits of wanting to go off and read alone.

The aims and values of school with regard to experiencing literature may well be at odds with those of the community. Perhaps, then, the use of picture story books as the major (if not the only) materials for early reading will not be based on anything the child has learnt at home. On the other hand, children (like Dominic) from homes where the sharing of books has been a major feature of life will be seeing immediate connections between home and the new world of the classroom. They will have experienced the power and will no doubt expect it from the new books read aloud by their teachers and found in the book corners. The same goes for poetry (or in the early years nursery and other rhymes), with some children arriving at school with a substantial repertoire and the knowledge that chanting together, delighting in language, and miming the actions is something adults and children do. If teaching is about building on and extending what children already know, using their present knowledge as a base, materials for teaching reading ought to reflect this. Perhaps for some children the cereal packet, nursery rhyme or advertising slogan would be a better early reading text than the stories set in the village of three corners or the walk undertaken by Rosie. The child who does not make progress quickly where 'reading books' are used may well have made progress with different materials. But the lack of progress can all too soon be perceived as a lack of 'ability' and then we (or rather the child) are set on a slippery path. Learning to read ought to be meaningful in the sense of it reflecting what a child thinks literacy to be about.

The text

While children are experiencing the power of story and rhyme and responding personally to them, they are also learning a great deal about how language and texts work. This was demonstrated in Chapter 2. The term 'literary competence' is often used to describe what readers learn about the 'rules' which operate in literary texts (Culler 1975). From reading poetry, for instance, we build up notions of how poetry works, so that faced with a new poem we know what sort of reading is likely to be involved. With very young children, we can examine a major aspect of literary competence through the stories they compose for us to scribe. Some children have learnt about story openings and endings, story characters and the sorts of things that happen to them. They know that stories are told in the past tense. Thomas's story in Chapter 2 demonstrates all of these features. However, as with expectations of what reading and writing are all about, there will always be a tremendous variation of such learning in any class of young children depending on their experiences at home.

We could, perhaps, extend the notion of literary competence at this stage of a reader's development to include what is being learnt about the language itself. Sharing hundreds of books at home in the pre-school years (for this is what many children do) will have drawn their attention to the alphabetic script which appears on the page. Again there will be variation in learning, from simply an awareness that the marks on the page tell the story to being able to recognize particular letters or words. This aspect of reading is not strictly the area we are concerned with in this book, but we must not forget the range of learning which can result from sharing books. Of course, knowledge about letters and words can also be gained from other sources, especially the environmental print which surrounds us all (Clark 1976; Goodman 1986).

Another fascinating area in which literature leads to learning about language is nursery rhymes. The delight in language which young children demonstrate when chanting, singing and learning by heart seems to be developing their sensitivity to language in ways which are important for their future reading development. Extending our notion of literary competence to include what young children are learning about the writing system, we find that experience of nursery rhymes teaches important reading lessons. First, and as a precursor to reading, the use of rhyme and alliteration in nursery rhymes leads to the development of phonological awareness – the realization that the words we speak are made up of sounds. As Goswami and Bryant (1991) write about their research in this area.

> We can be certain that children can detect rhyme and alliteration before they begin to read.

> The children's knowledge of nursery rhymes was strongly related to their sensitivity to rhyme two years later.

This sensitivity to the way in which language works seems to play an important role when children begin to learn to read:

> . . . a strong and specific relationship between the children's initial sensitivity to rhyme and alliteration and the progress that they made in learning to read and spell over the following three years.

> Rhyme makes an independent and distinctive contribution to reading.

The use of rhyme and alliteration in advertising jingles on television will surely be another source for the development of this phonemic awareness. Perhaps we need to make more use of such examples. Bedtime stories and nursery rhymes, however, have been features of the lives of pre-school children for a long, long time. The reasons for adults introducing them to and enjoying them with children have had little to do with the important 'reading lessons' which we now know they teach. Rather, there has been a desire to pass on something remembered as important from one's own childhood, something powerful which is mixed up with deep emotions and memories of people and homes. Part of the power of these early experiences of literature is that so often they are associated with having the attention of a loved adult and the chance to cuddle up and enjoy the physical closeness and the way the voice tells the story or sings the rhyme. Children who are lucky enough to have their early years full of such times go to school with great advantages in the business of learning to read and write. Not only have they realized that literature has a great deal to say to them about themselves – their fears, sadnesses, joys – but they have learnt a great deal about how language and written text words.

How do we find out?

If children are arriving at school with a great variety of experiences and awareness of reading, we surely ought to take this into account. The first question we need to ask, therefore, is 'Do we find out?' (closely followed by, 'If we do find out, does this assessment make any difference to our teaching of different children?'). The danger of teaching a set reading programme to each child regardless of where they are coming to reading from has been pointed out many times in the history of reading instruction, not least by Marie Clay (1991): 'It then becomes the responsibility of the school to arrange the early reading programme in ways that do not require all five-year-olds to fit a single shoe size'.

In terms of the focus of this book, finding out can involve:

● Home visiting. Discovering about the home literacies which children will bring to school means informed observation of where children are coming from. *Read It To Me Now*, by Hilary Minns (1990), is an invaluable resource for such work.

● Leaving a child alone with a picture story book and observing what happens. Does the child demonstrate 'reading behaviour', opening the book, turning the pages and following the story through the illustrations?

● Setting up play situations in which children can act as adults and 'read' or tell stories to each other or to dolls and observing what happens. Does the child do this? Does he or she tell the story suggested by the illustrations?

Does he or she know stories which have obviously come from home? Does he or she use a story voice with appropriate intonation?

- Sharing a book with the child and finding out what the child knows about how stories go (What do you think might happen now?) and about written text (Where is the story? Can you point out a word? Can you point out a letter? As in Marie Clay's 'sand and stone' tests). Through sensitive discussion, we can also discover whether such an activity has been a regular feature of home life.
- Acting as a scribe for a child to tell a favourite story. Kyle's telling of 'The Three Little Pigs', with its close following of the text and its dramatic intonation and changes of pace and volume, indicates immediately that he has great awareness of stories and how they work.
- Acting as a scribe for a child to compose a story. An analysis of its features will indicate what the child knows about the story and the written language of narrative. Not all children will be able to compose a story as long or as complex as that of Thomas in Chapter 2. Indeed, some children, who have little if any experience of story, will not be able to do this at all.
- Bringing in, and encouraging children to bring in, examples of environmental print – anything with print on it. While this has not been the focus of this book, we must not forget the learning which many children will have done in this area. Perhaps this would be a better way into reading for some children than story. The child who can recognize the names of different breakfast cereals has engaged in reading and learnt important lessons about how literacy works.

The above ideas are about assessing a child's reading development in order that we can best aid further development and help that child learn to read. They are time-consuming and the danger is that we neglect them in the rush to get on with our teaching. Then, when some children fail to make progress, we assume the reason lies in the child rather than the inappropriateness of what we have provided. Yet none of the above tasks, except the home visiting, is complex. Adults helping in classrooms can have them explained and carry them out for us. Discussion of the findings will be of benefit to all.

The early years at school (What do we do now that we have found out?)

Taking account of both sides of reading

Before looking at activities for the early years classroom, there needs to be a statement of what will underpin practice. This book has examined both sides of the reading process, the reader and the text, and we have argued that traditionally we have neglected the former. The various debates (and arguments!) about the teaching of initial reading have all focused on how readers deal with texts. Even the recognition that there is more to reading than the grapho-phonic code (important though that is) has still focused us on other aspects of text. Miscue analysis and running records recognize the complexity of reading by drawing our attention to semantic and syntactic cues, but these are just further aspects of how children make their way through texts. Comprehension in early reading (e.g. in reading tests such as the Neale Analysis) has assumed a one-way process in terms of gaining meaning from texts. Yet examples in previous chapters have made us realize the difficulty of talking about the meaning of a literary text. The danger is that our view of the reading of literature with young children is based simply on how it appears in such assessment procedures. Certainly, there is (or ought to be!) enough common understanding to agree on meaning at a surface level. *Jude the Obscure* is not about a woman who leads an expedition to the Amazon jungle. *Where the Wild Things Are* (Sendak 1967) is not about a bank holiday outing to Bognor. We could summarize each of these works in ways which would find agreement with most (all?) readers. Yet beyond such summaries of setting, plot and character, what do these stories mean to the different readers who engage with them? Why did the cricket commentator John Arlott describe *Jude the Obscure* as the greatest novel written in English? Why does *Where the Wild Things Are* cast such a powerful spell over young children? What meaning are these readers making for themselves? We can never know exactly, for the response lies deep in their minds and hearts, a mingling of memory, fear, hope, experience, personality. Surely in our teaching we need to recognize that there is more to the experience than how a child has managed to read a particular word, phrase or sentence, or answer questions such as 'What is that paragraph/page/chapter/verse about?':

> Anyone who has ever read stories to young children knows how deeply they can engage their feelings and how lasting an imprint they can have on their imaginations. If the world of young children is magical and numinous, it is not only because of the way they think, but also because of how they feel. A theory of development that requires us to leave fantasy behind is a limited tool for analyzing how we read literature.
>
> (Appleyard 1990)

Sharing books with children

A teacher spending time with a child who is reading a book aloud is instantly recognizable as a scene from life in the early years classroom. Most teachers see the organization of such times as a major (if not the major) aim of the school day. However, what might happen on such occasions varies widely, due both to the perception of the teacher as to their purpose and to the demands of large classes. At one end of a continuum the emphasis is very much on finding time to read, discuss and explore the text with the child, while at the other end is the desperate dash to 'hear' as many readers as possible in the shortest time. As one student teacher commented, 'My teaching practice teacher is really good. She can hear three readers at once'.

Even if a teacher knows that providing quality time is the aim, the sheer numbers of children involved makes the providing of that time very difficult. A study of 52 children aged between 5.6 and 7.4 years old (Hannon *et al.* 1986), who were heard reading both at home and at school, found that the mean duration of the sessions was 5 minutes and 30 seconds at home and 5 minutes and 5 seconds at school. However, those times were not devoted solely to the readers but were subjected to interruptions (mean interruptions per session: 0.77 at home and 2.71 at school).

So, in the classroom a short period of five minutes is interrupted nearly three times. Hardly the necessary conditions for exploring aspects of the text with a child let alone the child's response to the text. This book is not directly concerned with classroom organization and management and the issue has been raised here only because it can be an important factor in determining whether a teacher can do what he or she knows he or she ought to do. We know we ought to be spending time sharing books with children, but how do we do it with 30 other children clamouring for attention? Nevertheless, research into the ways teachers operate in classrooms (most recently the Leeds Primary Needs Survey, summarized in Alexander 1992) points to some teachers being much more successful than others. For some of us, interruptions are a major feature of our work, while others use strategies which minimize them. Allowing for the complexities of classroom life, perhaps one aim could be to ensure that each child reads with someone each day. This could be a classroom assistant, nursery nurse or adult helper. It could be carried out at home on a properly managed home–school programme. In addition, though, and regularly, the teacher will spend a longer period of time with a child. A second aim will be the sharing of books with groups of children and the whole class. These could be large-format books (Big Books) which enable each child to see the illustrations and the text. Lots of opportunities, then, both as individuals and with other children to engage with texts.

The second factor determining the quality of this work is the teacher's perception as to its purpose. Perhaps sometimes there is a confusion here between assessment and teaching. If the former is our aim, then letting a child read aloud to check on progress might be enough (given that we are sure what we are looking for). However, we would argue that the times when a child and a teacher find time together with a book are not just about assessment. Rather, they are the times when we can teach children to read. The same principle applies to working with large-format books and groups of children. We have argued above that we would want to explore both sides of the reading process with children as the basis of this teaching. Children need to learn about writing and texts in terms we outlined in Chapter 2, but they also need to know that we view reading as more than just the text. Their own responses to powerful writing must surely be explored and status (and time) given to their feelings, thoughts and comments. What might this look like in the classroom?

The following ideas are not to be taken as a set of tram lines but rather as suggestions for the sorts of things which could happen when we share a book with children. To begin with, we need to distinguish between whether the book is being read for the first time or has already been read on previous occasions. A first reading of any literary work will be different to further readings. Not only do we know what to expect but our response is influenced by our memory of how we felt the first time. Exactly how the readings differ will also depend on the text. Sometimes a first reading draws us close in to the action. We are so caught up in it that we are not particularly aware of how the text is working. A subsequent reading may be a more distanced reading so that we are more aware of the text itself rather than just what is happening. We will also pick up clues to later developments which we might have missed the first time round. These factors apply as much to young children with picture story books as to adults reading novels. They apply to poetry as much as to prose.

A first reading

Consider the title, author, illustrator, front cover – much as adults do when choosing what to read in a bookshop or library. Demonstrate that this is the typical behaviour of readers; that we have to make important decisions based on whether we think we will enjoy the book or not. The discussion will lead naturally into a consideration of what the book might be about, so do we have any idea?

Read the book aloud to the children – a dramatic reading which tries to draw them into the world of the story. A reading which we know is affecting them from the intense staring in their eyes, the held breath, the smiles and giggles at appropriate places. A first contact should be about what is happening and how this makes the reader feel. Children need to have clear expectations regarding the need for them to listen without interruption to this reading. They know full well the power of the connections readers make with texts and are desperate to inform us. However, constant interruptions of the 'I've got a kitten like that' or 'My dad does that' type can ruin the experience both for themselves and others. They need to be sure of the chance to have their say when the reading has finished.

Often when teachers share books with groups or the class, they auto-
matically begin by reading the text aloud. We believe that it is also a
powerful strategy when we are working with individual children. All too
often in our experience, children are only ever expected to read aloud text
which is new to them. If that text is constantly 'difficult' in the sense that we
try to provide reading materials which will 'stretch' the child, then reading
becomes a matter of simply getting through the words. It is very difficult to
get personally involved with a story if one is having difficulty reading it! Not
only, though, does an initial reading by us enable a child to focus on the
meaning and to respond to it, in addition it gives that child a 'map' of the
text so that when he or she has a go, he or she has some idea of how the
text goes (Meek 1988).

One aspect of reading aloud to young children which needs consideration is the effect the illustrations have on response. In Chapters 3 and 4,
we examined 'imaging' as an important part of response. Adult readers
(and older child readers) generally do not read illustrated texts. We form
our own 'pictures in the mind' turning the print on the page into personal
images of the places, characters and action. Picture books, by definition,
contain an illustrators' version of the text. The pictures do the work for us.
Of course, many of the most powerful picture story books produced for
children are not just illustrated versions of stories. In a Maurice Sendak or
an Antony Brown, the pictures and the text interact dynamically, the former not simply reflecting the text but adding new dimensions to it. Nevertheless, we would argue that regularly we ought to read aloud without
letting children see pictures, forcing them to produce their own in their
own minds. They can draw a character or a dramatic event, comparing
their ideas with those of others. They can then be shown the book's illustrations and make further comparisons.

Working with students and teachers on in-service courses, we have
used Hansel and Gretel to demonstrate the powerful ways in which illustrations influence our response to stories. The first half of the traditional tale
is read aloud and then discussed in terms of the pictures formed by the
listeners. Generally, these owe much to the traditional ways fairy tales have
been illustrated in the past, with the influence of Disney films (e.g. *Snow
White*) sometimes mentioned. Now the tale is read again, but this time
accompanied by Antony Brown's illustrations. These show the action taking
place initially in a modern setting with an all too real father and foster
mother. Suddenly, this tale takes on new and sinister overtones. No longer
are we distanced safely from it by virtue of its being a fairy tale set in a time
long, long ago. Now it is about real, present-day parents deciding to
murder their children. The effect on many of the adults we are working
with is marked. Some find the illustrations too much to bear. Often they
provoke anger and heated debate. Illustrations play a large part in the

reading experiences of young children. We need to be aware of their power and, perhaps, sometimes explore them with the children we teach.

Now we can discuss the text and we would want to emphasize the word 'discuss'. The danger is that we see our role as simply bombarding the children with a series of questions to ensure that they have understood what we believe to be the most important features of the text. Such oral comprehension tests soon give children the idea that this is the main aim of the exercise: we listen to and read books in order to answer questions on them. We can certainly recognize ourselves falling into this trap and have been there many times! But we think about it whenever we find ourselves reading aloud to children. With the original National Curriculum document stating that to achieve Level One, 'Speaking And Listening', a child had to 'Listen and respond to a range of stories . . .', the question, 'Well, how do I know if she has responded?', might lead to just such questions as those above. The first re-write states (in the section 'Response to Literature') that to achieve Level One a child has to 'Talk about the main features or events of a story or poem'. Again the focus is totally on the text and its perceived 'meaning', not on personal response at all.

A discussion, on the other hand, means just that. Not a series of questions from us, no matter how much we are itching to impose our reading on the child or group. We must emphasize that we are here considering an initial discussion following an initial reading. Exploration of the text will come later. When adults leave the theatre after *Romeo and Juliet* with tears in their eyes, or are moved and horrified by the poetry of Wilfred Owen or laugh aloud at the exploits of Lucky Jim, they are responding to what is being enacted or described. The techniques employed by the writers will be worth exploring later to see how it was done. First literature must cast its spell.

Rather than a question, then, a good way to start is to share our own enthusiasm for what has been read: 'Well, what a story! I really liked the bit where . . .'. In our experience, such a response from us leads almost immediately to an outpouring of comments from children. You can almost hear them muttering: 'So that's what it's all about. It's OK just to say what we enjoyed'. With a large group or the class the problem then becomes one of managing the situation! A way round this is to step back and realize that even with young children (perhaps especially with young children), the class discussion is very difficult. Children can appreciate this if we draw their attention to it, explaining that they cannot all talk at once, so initially they are going to talk in twos to the child next to them. This gives everyone the chance to have their say (just as it does with adults) and can then be developed into a teacher-led discussion. Our agenda for this will give children ideas for what they could be saying in their twos, so that the whole process is a 'drip-feed' approach, building up awareness over time.

Having enjoyed discussing the book we can now do some silent 'reading'. The children sit silently while we turn the pages. This is when they 'tell the story in their minds', engaging with the text and letting the illustrations take them through the action. A really magical aspect of a shared reading which, again, is equally applicable to the child on their own with us. Eventually for all of us reading is a silent activity, the reader and the text alone and quiet. This is the chance for children, just starting out on the road that hopefully will lead to lifelong reading, to behave like grown up readers.

Subsequent readings

Initial response, then, should focus on the meaning of the text – what has happened – and the ways it has affected the reader. Children love reading and listening to books they enjoy, often over and over again when much of the attraction for the adult has worn a bit thin. In the same way, adults will return to poetry which is important to them and even novels (and certainly to music – it would be thought most odd to say, 'I've heard that once, so no point in listening again'). Examples of people regularly re-reading particular novels or the works of particular writers are not uncommon. These subsequent readings will be different to first encounters with texts as discussed above. With young children, they are a chance to move from a focus on what happened and how we felt to an exploration of aspects of the text.

First, we need to recall that first reading. Who can remember the title/author/illustrator? Who can remember what happened? Who can remember how we felt? We establish the excitement again, the power of the experience. Perhaps the 'silent reading' described above can take place again as a reminder to the children.

Now the book can be read aloud again, but this time with the child or children encouraged to join in. Some books have obvious aspects of the text which enable this to happen. Poetry with strong rhythm and rhyme works especially well and the importance of phonemic awareness has already been discussed. The repetition of particular words, phrases or sentences can be emphasized as in *A Dark, Dark Tale*, which we examined in Chapter 2. Sometimes there are the almost ritualistic parts which can be changed together: 'Who's been eating my porridge?' said Daddy Bear. 'Who's been eating my porridge?' said Mummy Bear. 'Who's been eating my porridge? said Baby Bear, 'And . . .!' Sometimes it is just a repeated refrain: 'Not now Bernard'. The reading really is shared at this stage, and as popular books are read over and over again, so children can join in with more of the text.

As children get to know a book, it can be used to draw their attention to aspects of how texts work. Throughout this book we have seen response as having two sides, a reader and a text, and have argued for the demands of the text to be recognized and for children to be helped in their development as readers, able to cope with increasingly demanding texts. In the early years, this 'literary competence' encompasses both the 'big shapes' of story, plot, characters, openings and endings as well as aspects of how written language works. A great deal of this learning will be unconscious, children developing awareness simply through their contact with many texts. The stories they are able to tell demonstrate this learning (as we saw in Chapter 2). However, we can draw out aspects of text for consideration, drawing children's attention to them quite explicitly. The fact that they come from texts which are meaningful to them and which they have enjoyed and got to know means there is a better chance of this work making sense.

An example of work on 'big shapes' comes from a mixed age class of reception and year 1 children at Coniston Primary School in Cumbria (this work was first described in the journal *Reading*, 27(1), April 1973). The teacher, Wendy Yates, first got the children to survey the opening sentences of the books in the book corner. A list of the 'best' was compiled on large sheets of sugar paper and a number of sessions were spent discussing them. Then each child chose an opening for his or her own story. Wendy now demonstrated to the children how to plan a story, using a simple brainstorm technique. This is the plan of five-year-old George:

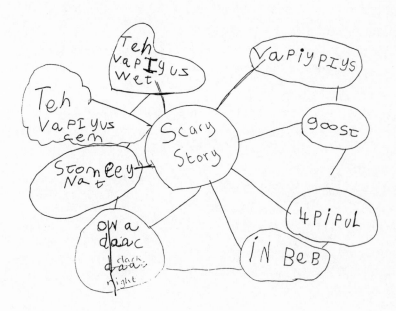

The children then wrote their story. George had particularly enjoyed Ruth Brown's *A Dark, Dark, Tale* and chose the opening line for his own story:

The Peepul Sreed and Sreed
Wen The vupiyus caam
Te yTod Ter Mummy
Mummy Tud
in To a gosT and
Sed vagfys
The vagiys weTTo mum

on a darK dark nighT The Vampires
starT To Cum daan the seeT
we NThe PeePuL wvr
in Bed. + PeePuL WVr
far a Seep. mon i SaaTf
To CUM. The PeePuL
Wo cup and The Vampiys
Cam

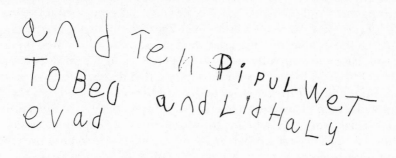

Each child was then paired with a year 2 child to produce a copy of the story on the word processor. The older child was encouraged to help the writer edit the text:

```
on   a   dark   dark     night    the
vampires  start  to  come  daan  the  seet
when  the    peepul  wur   in     bed  .  4
peepul   wur   fast   a   sleep.      monst
started   to   come  .The   peepul   woc
up  and  the  vampiys  came.  the
peepul   screemed   and   screemed  when
the  vampiyus  came  .  they  tode  ther
mummy.mummy  turned  into  a  gost  and
sed  vapiys  go  .the  vampiys  went  to
mum  and  the  pipul  went  to  bed  and
lived  happly  ev  aft.

BY  GEORGE  COOPER
```

Throughout the process, there was much discussion about how these stories might develop. Apart from the tremendous quality of the work itself for a reception child, it is impressive to note that George worked on his story for nearly three weeks.

Another important aspect of the growth of 'literary competence' in its widest sense is the establishment of the alphabetic principle and the development of knowledge of words, letters and sounds. We see this fitting clearly into our model of response but would emphasize that, as with the work on openings described above, its place is after a consideration of what the reader thinks and feels. Just as repetitive parts of a text can be highlighted for children to join in the reading, so words and sub-word units can be explored. Word searches can be enjoyed: 'That's the word for "bear", now if I turn over can you see it on this page?' Beginnings and endings of words can be examined at the level of syllables, onsets and rimes, prefixes and suffixes, letters and phonemes. If we were looking for words ending in 'ing', they can be found in a book, others added to a list displayed in the classroom, others searched for at home and brought in to school. Finally, they can be used to compose a poem which draws attention to the way they rhyme. Such work surely ought to be viewed as an important aspect of literary competence rather than as a separate 'skill area' to be approached in isolation from the sharing of and responding to powerful texts.

We would emphasize that the above ideas apply equally to poetry as they do to story books. Indeed, research by Goswami and Bryant (1991) would suggest that rhyme and rhythm ought to figure as a major thrust of early years literacy programmes. An invaluable book which explores how poetry can be approached is *Poetry 5–8* by Brian Merrick and Jan Balaam (1990). Chapter 5 examined advertising, and the use of jingles from television is another excellent resource. Nowadays, much as it might make us pause for thought, young children are perhaps more likely to know the words of the television advertising jingle than those of a traditional nursery rhyme. Finally, although not the remit of this book, we must not forget the print environment in which children grow up, as a resource for such work. Packets and tins and T-shirts and carrier bags can all provide meaningful texts on which to base reading in the classroom. Whatever the text, the same approach as that described in detail for picture story books will ensure that a rich awareness of what it means to share and respond to text will be made available to the children we teach.

Beyond the early stages

Work with children beyond the early stages develops from that described above. We would argue that the same pattern should apply: a consideration of personal response leading to an examination of how texts work. Again we wonder whether the former has been recognized sufficiently in the classroom. A glance through the questions which are set in English course books on poems or extracts from novels almost always shows the focus to be entirely on the meaning of the text, the way the text works and the meaning of particular words and phrases. The same goes for the proposed SAT at the end of Key Stage Two. It could be argued that only the text and its surface meaning can be explored and that to attempt to assess personal response would be unworkable. The danger with such an argument lies in the well-known effect which assessment has on teaching. If no mention is made of personal response in the assessment, then this area achieves little status in the classroom. Course books follow assessment requirements ('Covers all the attainment levels and helps prepare your pupils for the SAT') and so teachers who rely on such books for their work will not be guided towards the part the reader plays in reading. Children soon get the message that their thoughts and feelings do not count. What matters is to know what this word means, why that character behaved in a particular way or why this line is 'effective' (whether they think it is or not!). Of course, exploring personal response can be a difficult and sensitive area. We might be moved by a poem or story, know full well why we have been moved but not wish to share the reasons with anyone else.

Some years ago one of us taught a boy, Sean, who had a social welfare file as thick as a telephone directory. Gene Kemp's (1979) novel *The Turbulent Term of Tyke Tyler* was being read aloud to the class and Sean would often stay behind afterwards to talk about it. Why he focused in particular on Tyke's friend Danny was obvious, knowing Sean's background, but it was never made explicit by either Sean or his teacher. Perhaps, in general, we have the responsibility to let children know how we respond to the stories and poems we share with them. We ought to be able to talk about how they make us think and feel. Some children may then feel confident enough about describing their own thoughts and feelings. Others will not, but this does not matter. They will be realizing that literature does affect people in powerful ways and that this is an important part of reading.

Exploring response: Using a short story

The work we described in Chapters 3 and 4 was an attempt to examine how readers read literature. We used the openings of novels and poems and encouraged adults and children to write down whatever was going through their minds as they read them. Our resulting model of the reading process contains features which come from the reader and features which refer to aspects of the text. We now need to consider how we might explore this model with children in classrooms. In terms of prose, the short story offers the chance to do so and has a number of advantages over full-length novels. First, the whole work can be read in a single session with everyone in the class experiencing it together. Second, if a range of short stories are used over time, there is a good chance of every child finding at least one they enjoy. While reading a novel aloud to the class over some weeks is a popular activity (and something we have enjoyed doing ourselves many times), we must not forget the children who are not enjoying our particular choice and see it stretching ahead of them for weeks. The one drawback to the short story is that it does not allow for the development of characters over time. In a full-length novel, characters may change as a result of experiences or even grow from children into adults and one of the pleasures of reading is to witness this development. However, alongside the 'study' of short stories in class we would see children reading a range of novels and stories for themselves and being given help to discuss this reading with us and with each other. They will need an agenda to do so, for it is not at all obvious what we might talk about when asked to discuss something we have read. The danger is that as teachers we revert to something dimly remembered from our own work for GCE English literature rather than a model which reflects the two sides of the reading process.

The model suggested below has been used with children in classrooms, students on literature courses and teachers on in-service courses. We certainly would not recommend its use every time we read aloud to or with children. In the primary classroom, perhaps the most common strategy will be simply to provide a dramatic reading and allow the tale to work its magic. However, we also would want children to be developing their awareness of what is involved in the reading of literature, both in terms of how readers respond and how texts work. The ideas outlined below are aimed at developing that awareness which children will then take to their own reading.

1. Before you begin – What are your expectations?

Readers come to any text with expectations. These might be based on our knowledge of the author ('I always enjoy Roald Dahl'), the genre ('I always enjoy science fiction'), the reviews ('The greatest English novel this decade!'), the title ('Five Run Away To Kirrin Island Yet Again'), the cover (a young handsome couple in regency dress embracing passionately under a storm tossed tree), the length ('500 pages! I'll look for something shorter'). Sometimes we have expectations based on a number of these factors, while at other times we really are taking a risk when we embark on a new novel. The short story can be introduced in terms of its title, author and length. How much further information is provided will depend on our judgement of the story and the group with which we are working. The initial discussions always take place in pairs or small groups and then comments taken to get a feel for the initial expectations. There is always a range from the positive through the indifferent to the negative (whether we are working with children or adults!).

The session now follows a pattern in which some of the story is read and then a question provides a focus for group discussions. These lead to consideration of interesting points by the class as a whole.

2. Clues in the text – What is this going to be about?

The work on the openings of novels showed how powerfully readers try to predict what might be going to happen. Discussion here will focus on the setting (both time and place) and whether they are established. Are characters introduced? Does anything happen or is anything said which might provide clues as to future developments. Do we know yet what sort of a story this is going to be?

3. Pictures in the mind – How much from the text? How much from you?

The simple request to young children, 'Shut your eyes. What do you see?', is equally effective with older children and adults. As we showed in earlier chapters, the imaging which takes place when we read – converting the print on the page into pictures in our minds – certainly owes a lot to the text. After all, a great deal of the writer's craft is to create people, places and events for us to enjoy. However, readers bring their own memories and experiences to the business of reading and these influence the ways they 'see' what the writer is trying to describe. In addition, we view the action from particular standpoints, 'spectating' on what is happening (Harding 1977). The differences here between readers are often surprising and fascinating, especially where both adults and children are involved. We frequently see the action from the viewpoint of a particular character and this can provoke interesting discussion.

4. Predicting – What do you think will happen?

By this stage, enough of the story will have been read to allow for some thoughts as to the outcomes. What we think will happen is based on what we have read so far, so that it involves a looking back at the text. More clues of the sort discussed in (2) above will be discovered. Indeed, we have found that throughout this whole exercise both children and adults naturally refer back to the text. We do not have to 'force' them to do so. Predicting will also be influenced by our previous reading of similar texts. Ten-year-old Michelle did not think that the heroine, Poll, in Nina Bawden's (1975) novel *The Peppermint Pig*, would die from scarlet fever because 'In books they don't normally die half way through'.

5. Involvement – What do you want to happen?

Predicting works at two levels when we read. We rationally think things through as described above but this is not enough. With some novels, our involvement means that we become emotionally involved with a character or characters so that no matter what we 'think' is going to happen we desperately 'want' a particular outcome ('Oh please don't marry him'). How often in Hardy do we know that plans will not work out (because it is Hardy) but we still hope deep down that they will? How many readers, re-reading *Jude the Obscure* and therefore knowing the dreadful, tragic ending still find themselves wishing (hoping?) for alternatives? Of course, we cannot expect every reader to be as involved with every book they read and therefore must be prepared for indifference as the response at this point. However, discussion about why some do have hopes while others could not really care draws attention again to the active role of the reader and can make for interesting discussion.

6. After reading – Did it match your expectations?

The story has now been completed and we need to reflect on it. Initially, this means recalling the expectations discussed at the beginning of the reading and seeing whether the actual story matched them. We can explore aspects of the story which surprised any of the readers.

7. Connections with you: As a person? As a reader?

Here we explain the ways in which we bring a great deal of ourselves to what we read. In the case of personal connections, we now enter a very sensitive area and the example of Sean above draws our attention to it. We have suggested that we provide our own examples in the first instance in order to demonstrate this important aspect of reading. What we get from the groups will vary tremendously – sometimes nothing at all, sometimes superficial (though important) statements such as 'It's just like my own front room'. Sometimes, however, a comment or longer description results, which can be very moving and which reminds us of the power of what we read.

8. Would you change it in any way?

Children, especially, enjoy considering the 'improvements' they would make to the stories they read. Sometimes this results in alternative versions with major changes. Openings can be the focus: 'It was a bit slow to get going. I'd have it more exciting at the start'. Often endings are discussed with new scenarios described or the story is continued with additional scenes. It is here that general discussion of what people think of the story takes place. Was it a good read? Why? Would you recommend it to anyone else? The areas which this activity has focused on provide the agenda and we need to draw attention to them in order that discussion does not simply consist of a series of 'I just liked it'.

Every child in a class can join in the work described above. The short story is read in bits and we can read it aloud for all to be involved regardless of reading ability. The children follow copies of the text so that they have it for reference during their discussions. What is fascinating is how they do so in order to search for clues and justify their opinions and feelings. The aim is to provide a framework which enables children to discuss their reading of stories and novels. It demonstrates that there is more to reading than the answering of comprehension questions and that the personal responses of readers are worthy of discussion. Using the framework with a number of short stories will help children develop awareness of how texts work, which they can take to their own silent reading be it at school or at home.

Poetry

The work with very young children was equally applicable to both story and poetry, but with older children a slightly different approach is necessary. The aim remains the same – to explore both sides of the reading process – and a recognition of the powerful and personal ways in which we respond to poetry will lie at the heart of our work. Connections with ourselves and our own lives pervade our reading of poetry just as they do of stories and novels, and can be explored with sensitivity. Again, we need to provide the impetus by making explicit the connections which are important to us. Another common element is imaging, the pictures we create in our minds, and these can form the basis of fascinating discussions. Both of these aspects of the reading process were seen to be important in our work with adults and children described in Chapter 4.

For our child readers, though, poetry seemed to present difficulties which showed up in their comments and these hinged on the nature of poetry itself. There were many examples of children asking questions of the poems, seemingly puzzled by what they were reading: 'Who is he?', 'Why did he do that?', 'What school?'.

We saw 'gaps' as lying behind these questions. Both stories and poetry contain gaps in the text which the reader has to fill. Language cannot possibly describe something totally photographically, and this indeterminacy draws readers into the text. However, in poetry, there are far more gaps. A poem, by its very nature, is concentrated, pared down to the basics. To take one example, we can consider the background information which novelists provide about characters. As we read a novel, we expect this information and use it to build up a picture of the people we are reading about. We expect to learn something of what they look like: their ages, their circumstances, their personalities and their relationships. Poetry, however, rarely provides such information. Even poems which appear to be very detailed and which tell a story actually provide far less information to the reader than they would get in a novel. Experienced readers of poetry accept this and give it little thought when they read poetry. They have learnt what reading poetry is all about. As Jonathan Culler (1975) states: 'The poeticalness lies not in the poem as much as in the conventions which operate when we read on the assumption that a text is a piece of poetry'.

Apart from the way in which a poem 'stands alone' and has to be accepted as such, poetry makes more use of 'poetic techniques'. Again, this makes it different to a story. In 'Timothy Winters' we learn that 'Through his britches the blue winds blow' and the use of 'blue' means that we are dealing with a form of writing in which meaning is at one remove from the words on the page. As one child wrote next to this line: 'Blue winds? But you can't see the wind!' These differences between poems and stories have implications for classroom practice.

1. We read poems more than once

Young children will re-read the same picture book many, many times as any parent who has tried to suggest something different to the current favourite will testify. The length of novels means that older children and adults do not do nearly so much re-reading, although the popularity of series can be seen as simply reading the same book dressed up in different clothes. Details may change but basically the books in the series are almost indistinguishable. Read one book from the series and you have read them all. Indeed, Mills and Boon books are written to a strict formula. However, although we may return to a particular favourite at times, in general we move on from one novel to the next. But not with poetry. In this sense, poetry is like music, for not only do we return to the same work over and over again but our response to it changes over time. Sometimes it deepens so that only after a number of readings or listenings do we really appreciate the power of the work. Sometimes an initial enthusiasm palls and we find that something which seemed to mean so much to us now leaves us cold and indifferent. We fast-forward the tape or turn the page.

We appreciate that a first reading of a poem or a first listening to some music is not a good basis for saying that we 'know' it. Indeed, with complex works, perhaps we never can say that. One of the fascinations of any of the arts is that we can never tie them down and explain them fully. There is always something going on just beyond the language we are using to describe them. In the classroom, we would suggest this means that poems need to be read more than once before being discussed. The plethora of questions asked by our child readers were written during a first reading as they tried to sort out the conventions which were operating. Repeated readings give children the chance to accept the poem: 'So that's it. That's how it goes'. A strategy of reading the same poem first thing each morning and then discussing it on Friday means that children have had a chance to sort it out a little in their minds.

2. Discussion rather than questions

Discussion involves asking questions of the text, but we would want to encourage children to ask their own questions. The danger of using poetry as an excuse for a battery of comprehension questions is that we turn children into passive readers waiting to answer someone else's questions (in addition, these questions are often asked after just one reading). Discussion means pairs and groups of children faced with a poem which they have heard a number of times. Our role is to help establish an agenda which enables them to talk about it and this agenda will contain elements from both sides of the reading process. So we will give status to our own responses – connections with ourselves, our lives, the people we know, our thoughts, opinions and feelings. Looking at aspects of the text is an arid exercise if it does not spring from a consideration of how the poet managed to affect us so powerfully. At university, students studying literature will have to analyse many works which leave them cold. But, hopefully, they have arrived at the point where literature means so much to them that a study of it in its own right is worthwhile. They want to know about as much of it as possible simply because it is literature. They will have reached this point, however, through reading works which affected them deeply in childhood and adolescence. We are dealing with primary school children here and the great danger is that we forget the affective in our misguided obsession with a watered-down version of literary criticism. We can draw the attention of children to the ways poems work, but if we want to turn children into readers who both can and do read we need to establish in the primary years that poetry has something to say to them as people. The danger of producing the 'technique spotters' discussed in Chapter 5 is real enough in secondary schools; primary children should be developing a love of poetry first and foremost.

Advertising: Resisting the text

As we suggested in Chapter 5, the process of responding to adverts has much in common with that of responding to literature. Again there are two sides to the process, a reader and a text, and advertisers certainly take both into account in their work. The connections they would have us make between ourselves and the product, and the projection of an idealized lifestyle for us if we use the product, demonstrate their awareness of the part played by the reader. Their use of a range of techniques from poetry and narrative show how carefully they craft the text. We are not suggesting that the experience of reading, say, a Shakespearean sonnet is no different to that of an advertisement for the latest sports car (although there could be much debate around such a suggestion!), simply that the same process appears to be going on. The reader will be bringing a great deal of her/ himself to the reading and the text will be constructed to affect us in particular ways.

We have argued for the importance of the way readers are drawn into literary text, especially stories, and of the power of the resulting experience.

The work described above moves from a consideration of our thoughts and feelings, provoked by the text, into an examination of how the text manages to affect us. Perhaps the same sort of approach is equally applicable to adverts. Three of the stages we described for a consideration of a short story form the structure for discussing them.

1. Expectations

If a number of motor car adverts are to be examined, it is worth exploring what children would expect them to be like. Their expectations are rarely wrong, they already having a good idea what the advertisers will want to emphasize. Nevertheless, emphases change so that present concerns with safe, 'green' vehicles may come as a surprise.

2. Clues in the text – How do they work?

Here we discuss two aspects of text. First, the type of text itself. Is it very obviously an advert or (as we saw in Chapter 5) does it purport to be a story or even a poem? What do we think lies behind this choice? How is it arranged on the page? What is the relationship between the text and illustration? How do we 'read' the illustration (shapes, colours, images)? As with stories and poetry, we would emphasize the need for this to be a discussion, initially in pairs or small groups. When we draw ideas together in a class discussion, the agenda would emerge and can be developed in future sessions.

The second aspect of text would be a close examination of the language used. The basic questions are 'What sort of effect is the advert trying to have on the reader?' and 'How is the language being used to have this effect?' We are very close here to the ways we examine the language of poetry. However, a week spent collecting examples of one area of advertising (e.g. that produced by estate agents) enables us to focus in some detail on the use of language. All of the words which are trying to 'sell' the product can be listed and discussed. Similarly, the poetic techniques of, for example, rhyme, rhythm, assonance, alliteration, simile and metaphor can be highlighted. Here the similarities and differences to poetry begin to appear. While the poet aims at a use of language which describes exactly what he or she is describing, thinking or feeling, the advertiser often uses language deliberately vaguely ('the best', 'perfect', 'good'). The techniques may be the same and there may be an equal awareness of how language can be shaped for effect, but in reality the poet and the marketing executive are not engaged in the same activity. The one is aiming at precision while the other only appears to be doing so.

3. Connections with you?

Just as we bring so much of ourselves to the reading of literature, so we do so with adverts. This can range from recognizing ourselves ('She's just like me, trying to get the family washing as clean as possible'), through guilt ('If I want to be a good mother I ought to use that washing powder') to wishful thinking ('If I use that washing powder I am in some way connected with that ideal family being shown'). Adverts can show us what we think we are, what we think we ought to be and what we would like to be. Making explicit to children these techniques not only provokes lively debate, but is so important in educating children in something which plays and will play such an important part in their lives. How amazing that reference to the 'reading' of advertising disappeared in the first re-write of the National Curriculum English document.

Reading in the primary classroom: Teachers as readers

Underlying all of the work described above is a notion of the teacher as a reader who is enthusiastic about the world of reading. For these teachers, the key is simply to share their enthusiasm so that it rubs off on the children they teach. In doing so, they need to trust themselves and think about what turned them into readers and why they continue to read as adults. The danger is the separation of their own enthusiasm from the work they give to children in the classroom. One teacher on an in-service course which had considered the sorts of issues raised in this book spoke movingly (and not a little sadly) about her many years teaching during which she had not thought that her joy in reading at home had any relevance to her teaching of primary children. To a non-specialist, the agenda of the course book and the work sheet plus memories of 'O' level English literature had suggested an approach to reading with nine-year-olds which she ought to be following. She now recognized that the reasons why she read would stand a better chance of turning her children into readers.

Even if we are not readers at home, we need to ensure that we know something of the books we expect children to read (indeed, have read many of them) in order that we can share the experience with them and make suggestions as to what they might enjoy. The National Curriculum contains lists of popular authors as a basic guideline and time to read them can be found very simply by instituting silent reading sessions every day when both teachers and children read. In one year, any teacher can read a range of fiction and poetry while also demonstrating reading to children (20 minutes a day is approximately 60 hours reading in a school year!). In our experiences, a major challenge for headteachers and English curriculum coordinators in primary schools is to address the scene (still common) of children standing in front of shelves of novels with no basis for deciding what to choose other than a piece of coloured tape on the spines of the books. Before we can engage in stimulating work with children, we do have to read what they are reading.

A report entitled *How in the World Do Students Read?* was produced in 1993 by the International Association for the Evaluation of Educational Achievement. It gave the results of a survey of reading standards of children aged nine and fourteen in 32 countries. Some 200 000 children were surveyed. In the report, they give a description of the features of teachers who achieve high reading standards with children and paint a picture of the 'successful reading teacher' of nine-year-olds:

> The good teacher of reading for nine year olds . . . is very experienced and reads a lot herself . . . She gives the children plenty of opportunity for independent, silent reading and often holds discussions about the books they have read . . . Her pupils are encouraged to read outside school and use the library often . . . During reading lessons they are guided to make sense of the text by relating it to their own experiences, by predicting what is going to happen next and by making generalisations and inferences.

In this book, we have focused on the ways readers respond to texts and have suggested strategies in the primary classroom for helping children develop as readers. The classroom work has come from these responses so that we have argued for more status to be given to the very personal ways in which readers are affected by what they read. Examining how different texts work needs to proceed from how they manage to exert such a powerful spell on readers. We stand back from a text to answer questions such as 'How does it make me think or feel in these ways?' and 'How does it work or not work?' Certainly with primary children, analysis of texts for its own sake is unlikely to create the excitement for reading that we would see as our prime aim. Excitement can also result from the many imaginative activities which have been a feature of the best primary practice for many years: dramatizing extracts, interviews with characters, designing alternative dust jackets, illustrating key scenes, giving dramatic readings, etc. These re-creation activities can be found in many excellent books and articles. Certainly, we would recommend such activities as a major feature of primary work. We have not focused on them simply because they are now so well established. However, we would argue for children also to discuss texts in the ways we have suggested if they are to share their responses and develop awareness of how they work.

We have focused on both literature and advertising, suggesting that a similar process is going on in each. The difference is how far we want to be drawn as readers into the texts which are created. We want to finish the book with literature. While we are fascinated with the ways language is used by the media, it was as readers of stories and poetry that we began this work. In 1983 at Birmingham University on a course concerned with the teaching of English, Emrys Evans, the course tutor suggested four principles for the teaching of literature. In our work with the adult and child readers over the past couple of years, we have found ourselves drawn back to these principles, whether we were dealing with pre-school children at home gazing at a picture book or with adults struggling with the opening of a Martin Amis novel or a poem by Gerard Manley Hopkins. We would like to finish our book with them.

1. Pleasure and involvement precede full understanding.
2. Each reader's encounter with any text produces a unique experience. It is no part of the teacher's business to reduce that uniqueness to uniformity.
3. Literature is, however, a social phenomenon. Therefore, a text can be shared and discussed.
4. Such discussion is the foundation of criticism.

Three-year-old Dominic, then (in Chapter 2), with his father engaged in the beginnings of literary criticism. We would want to argue for the development of this in the primary classroom, pushing aside memories of 'O' level literary criticism and with them the traditional comprehension questions of so many English course books. In their place, children discussing stories, novels and poems because of the powerful effects they have on them as people and as readers. Our task, as primary teachers, is to provide them with agendas for such discussions.

The Remains of the Day (Kazuo Ishiguro)

It seems increasingly likely that I really will undertake the expedition that has been preoccupying my imagination now for some days. An expedition, I should say, which I will undertake alone, in the comfort of Mr Farraday's Ford; an expedition which, as I foresee it, will take me through much of the finest countryside of England to the West Country, and may keep me away from Darlington Hall for as much as five or six days. The idea of such a journey came about, I should point out, from a most kind suggestion put to me by Mr Farraday himself one afternoon almost a fortnight ago, when I had been dusting the portraits in the library. In fact, as I recall, I was up on the step-ladder dusting the portrait of Viscount Wetherby when my employer had entered carrying a few volumes which he presumably wished returned to the shelves. On seeing my person, he took the opportunity to inform me that he had just that moment finalized plans to return to the United States for a period of five weeks between August and September. Having made this announcement, my employer put his volumes down on a table, seated himself on the *chaise-longue*, and stretched out his legs. It was then, gazing up at me, that he said:

'You realize, Stevens, I don't expect you to be locked up here in this house all the time I'm away. Why don't you take the car and drive off somewhere for a few days? You look like you could make good use of a break.'

Coming out of the blue as it did, I did not quite know how to reply to such a suggestion. I recall thanking him for his . . .

London Fields (Martin Amis)

This is a true story but I can't believe it's really happening.
It's a murder story, too. I can't believe my luck.

And a love story (I think), of all strange things, so late in the century, so late in the goddamned day.

This is the story of a murder. It hasn't happened yet. But it will. (It had better.) I know the murderer, I know the murderee. I know the time, I know the place. I know the motive (*her* motive) and I know the means. I know who will be the foil, the fool, the poor foal, also utterly destroyed. And I couldn't stop them, I don't think, even if I wanted to. The girl will die. It's what she always wanted. You can't stop people, once they *start.* You can't stop people, once they *start creating.*

What a gift. This page is briefly stained by my tears of gratitude. Novelists don't usually have it so good, do they, when something real happens (something unified, dramatic and pretty saleable), and they just write it down?

I must remain calm. I'm on deadline too here, don't forget. Oh, the pregnant agitation. Someone is tickling my heart with delicate fingers. Death is much on people's minds.

Three days ago (is it?) I flew in on a red-eye from New York. I practically had the airplane to myself. I stretched out, calling piteously and frequently to the stewardesses for codeine and cold water. But the red-eye did what a red-eye does. Oh, my. Jesus, I look . . .

North and South (Mrs Gaskell)

CHAPTER 1
'Haste to the Wedding'

'Wooed and married and a'.'

'Edith!' said Margaret gently, 'Edith!'

But as Margaret half suspected, Edith had fallen asleep. She lay curled up on the sofa in the back drawing-room in Harley Street, looking very lovely in her white muslin and blue ribbons. If Titania had ever been dressed in white muslin and blue ribbons, and had fallen asleep on a crimson damask sofa in a back drawing-room, Edith might have been taken for her. Margaret was struck afresh by her cousin's beauty. They had grown up together from childhood, and all along Edith had been remarked upon by every one, except Margaret, for her prettiness; but Margaret had never thought about it until the last few days, when the prospect of soon losing her companion seemed to give force to every sweet quality and charm which Edith possessed. They had been talking about wedding dresses, and wedding ceremonies; and Captain Lennox, and what he had told Edith about her future life at Corfu, where his regiment was stationed; and the difficulty of keeping a piano in good tune (a difficulty which Edith seemed to consider as one of the most formidable that could befall her in her married life), and what gowns she should want in the visits to Scotland, which would immediately succeed her marriage; but the whispered tone had latterly become more drowsy; and Margaret, after a pause of a few minutes, found, as she fancied, that in spite of the buzz in the next room, Edith had rolled herself up into a soft ball of muslin and ribbon, and silken curls, and gone off into a peaceful little after-dinner nap.

Margaret had been on the point of telling her cousin of some of the plans and visions which she entertained as to her future life in the country parsonage, where her father and mother lived; and where her bright holi-days had always been passed, though for the last ten years her aunt Shaw's house had been considered . . .

The Eighteenth Emergency (Betsy Byers)

The pigeons flew out of the alley in one long swoop and settled on the awning of the grocery store. A dog ran out of the alley with a torn Cracker Jack box in his mouth. Then came the boy.

The boy was running hard and fast. He stopped at the sidewalk, looked both ways, saw that the street was deserted and kept going. The dog caught the boy's fear, and he started running with him.

The two of them ran together for a block. The dog's legs were so short he appeared to be on wheels. His Cracker Jack box was hitting the sidewalk. He kept glancing at the boy because he didn't know why they were run-ning. The boy knew. He did not even notice the dog beside him or the trail of spilled Cracker Jacks behind.

Suddenly the boy slowed down, went up some steps and entered an apartment building. The dog stopped. He sensed that the danger had passed, but he stood for a moment at the bottom of the steps. Then he went back to eat the Cracker Jacks scattered on the sidewalk and to snarl at the pigeons who had flown down to get some.

Inside the building the boy was still running. He went up the stairs three at a time, stumbled, pulled . . .

Run for Your Life (David Line)

I

It was a rainy day in November when I met him first, and about a regiment of them seemed to be bashing him. He was a little dark skinny lad who looked about eight, but I knew he couldn't be because of the school cap. It was our school cap, and we don't take kids under eleven. The cap was in a puddle, and so was this kid. He was down on his knees in it, and that's where they were bashing him.

As far as I could see, he was letting them. He wasn't struggling or yelling or anything. He was just kneeling there sobbing, and doing that pretty quietly.

I said, 'All right, break it up.'

It was dark in the alley and they had to peer at me.

'Get lost,' one of them said, uncertainly.

'Yeah, vanish.'

'Scramaroo.'

They let go of him all the same.

I could see they were younger than me, and smaller, which was all right except one of them had some kind of cosh in his hand, a piece of hosepipe or something.

'I know you!' this one yelled suddenly, just about the same moment I realized I knew him, too. He was a tough young kid with an elder brother who'd made my life a misery at another school. 'You're Woolcott, ain't you? I know where you live, Woolcott. Better shove off if you don't want trouble.'

'Yeah, shove.'

'Buzz off. He's ours.'

I said to the kid, 'Get up.'

The Worst Witch (Jill Murphy)

CHAPTER ONE

MISS CACKLE'S Academy for Witches stood at the top of a high mountain surrounded by a pine forest. It looked more like a prison than a school, with its gloomy grey walls and turrets. Sometimes you could see the pupils on their broomsticks flitting like bats above the playground wall, but usually the place was half hidden in mist, so that if you glanced up at the mountain you would probably not notice the building was there at all.

Everything about the school was dark and shadowy: long, narrow corridors and winding staircases – and of course the girls . . .

The Way to Sattin Shore (Philippa Pearce)

Chapter I

THE BEAM OF DARKNESS

Here is Kate Tranter coming home from school in the January dusk – the first to come, because she is the youngest of her family. Past the churchyard. Past the shops. Along the fronts of the tall, narrow terrace houses she goes. Not this one, nor this one, nor this . . .

Stop at the house with no lit window.

This is home.

Up three steps to the front door, and feel for the key on the string in her pocket. Unlock, and then in. Stand just inside the door with the door now closed, at her back.

Stand so, in the hall. Ahead, to the right, the stairs. Ahead, to the left, the passage to the kitchen: in the wider part, by the back door, a round, red, friendly eye has seen her – the reflector of her bicycle.

To the left of the hall, Granny's room.

Kate Tranter took a slow breath. She made herself ready to start across the floor to the stairs – to cross the dark beam that came from her grandmother's room through the gap where her grandmother's door stood ajar.

On a weekday, at this time, her grandmother's eyes were always turned to that door, as she sat in her room . . .

The Naughtiest Girl in the School (Enid Blyton)

Chapter I

THE NAUGHTY SPOILT GIRL

"You'll have to go to school, Elizabeth!" said Mrs. Allen. "I think your governess is quite right. You are spoilt and naughty, and although Daddy and I were going to leave you here with Miss Scott, when we went away, I think it would be better for you to go to school."

Elizabeth stared at her mother in dismay. What, leave her home? And her pony and her dog? Go and be with a lot of children she would hate! Oh no, she wouldn't go!

"I'll be good with Miss Scott," she said.

"You've said that before," said her mother. "Miss Scott says she can't stay with you any longer. Elizabeth, is it true that you put earwigs in her bed last night?"

Elizabeth giggled. "Yes," she said. "Miss Scott is so frightened of them! It's silly to be afraid of earwigs, isn't it?"

"It is much sillier to put them into somebody's bed," said Mrs. Allen sternly. "You have been spoilt, and you think you can do what you like! You are an only child, and we love you so much, Daddy and I, that I think we have given you too many lovely things, and allowed you too much freedom."

"Mummy, if you send me to school, I shall be so naughty there that they'll send me back home again," said Elizabeth, shaking her hair back.

She was a pretty girl with laughing blue eyes and fair hair. All her life she had done as she liked. Six governesses had come and gone, but not one of them had been able to make Elizabeth obedient or good-mannered!

Elidor (Alan Garner)
'Childe Rowland to the Dark Tower came —'

King Lear, act iii, sc. 4.

1. *Thursday's Child*

'All right,' said Nicholas. 'You're fed up. So am I. But we're better off here than at home.'

'It wouldn't be as cold as this,' said David.

'That's what you say. Remember how it was last time we moved? Newspapers on the floor, and everyone sitting on packing cases. No thanks!'

'We're spent up,' said David. 'There isn't even enough for a cup of tea. So what are we going to do?'

'I don't know. Think of something.'

They sat on the bench behind the statue of Watt. The sculptor had given him a stern face, but the pigeons had made him look as though he was just very sick of Manchester.

'We could go and ride on the lifts in Lewis's again,' said Helen.

'I've had enough of that,' said Nicholas. 'And anyway, they were watching us: we'd be chucked off.'

'What about the escalators?'

'They're no fun in this crowd.'

'Then let's go home,' said David. 'Hey, Roland, have you finished driving that map?'

Roland stood a few yards away, turning the handles of a street map. It was a tall machine of squares and wheels and lighted panels.

'It's smashing,' he said. 'Come and look. See this roller? It's the street index: each one has its own letter and number. You can find any street in Manchester: it's easy. Watch.'

Roland spun a wheel at the side of the map, and the index whirled round, a blur under the glass.

Bibliography

Alexander, R. (1992). *Policy and Practice in Primary Education.* London, Routledge.

Amis, M. (1989). *London Fields.* London, Jonathan Cape.

Appleyard, B. (1990). *Becoming a Reader.* Cambridge, Cambridge University Press.

Babbitt, N. (1991). How books don't always mean what the writers intended. *Children's Literature in Education, 22* (2) pp. 89–96.

Barthes, R. (1985).1 Day by day with Roland Barthes. In Blonsky, M. (ed.), *On Signs.* Baltimore, MD, Johns Hopkins University Press.

Bawden, N. (1975). *The Peppermint Pig.* London, Gollancz.

Benton, M. (1992). *Secondary Worlds: Literature Teaching and the Visual Arts.* Buckingham, Open University Press.

Benton, M. and Fox, G. (1985). *Teaching Literature Nine to Fourteen.* Oxford, Oxford University Press.

Blyton, E. (1973). *The Naughtiest Girl in the School.* London, Deans International.

Brown, R. (1983). *A Dark, Dark Tale.* London, Scholastic.

Bryant, P. and Bradley, L. (1985). *Children's Reading Problems.* Oxford, Blackwell.

Bryce Heath, S. (1983). *Ways with Words.* Cambridge, Cambridge University Press.

Byars, B. (1973). *The Eighteenth Emergency.* Harmondsworth, Penguin.

Byatt, A.S. (1990). *Possession.* London, Chatto and Windus.

Calvino, I. (1979). *If on a Winter's Night a Traveller* (translated 1981). London, Martin Secker and Warburg.

Causley, C. (1968). 'Timothy Winters'. In *Voices 2.* Harmondsworth, Penguin.

Causley, C. (1986). 'My Aunt Dora'. In *Secret Destinations.* London, Macmillan Papermac.

Centre for Policy Studies (1987). *English, Whose English.* London, CPS.

Chambers, A. (1985). *Booktalk.* London, The Bodley Head.

Clark, M. (1976). *Young Fluent Readers.* London, Heinemann.

Clarke, G. (1985). 'Overheard in County Sligo'. In *Selected Poems.* Manchester, Carcanet Press.

Clay, M.M. (1991). *Becoming Literate.* London, Heinemann.

Cox, B. (1992). *Cox on Cox.* London, Hodder and Stoughton.

Craggs, C.E. (1992). *Media Education in the Primary School.* London, Routledge.

Crago, H. (1985). 'The roots of response'. In Hunt, P. (ed.) (1990), *Children's Literature: The Development of Criticism.* London, Routledge.

Culler, J. (1975). *Structuralist Poetics.* London, Routledge and Kegan Paul.

Davis, L.J. (1987). *Resisting Novels: Ideology & Fiction.* London, Methuen.

Day, G. (1990). *Readings in Popular Culture.* London, Macmillan.

Department of Education and Science (1990). *English in the National Curriculum.* London, HMSO.

Eliot, T.S. (1922). *The Waste Land.* London, Faber and Faber.

Fowler, R. (1986). *Linguistic Criticism.* Oxford, Oxford University Press.

Frame, J. (1982). *To the Is-Land.* London, Paladin.

Garner, A. (1965). *Elidor.* London, Collins.

Gaskell, E. (1854/1970). *North and South.* Harmondsworth, Penguin.

Giovanni, N. (1988). 'a heavy rap'. In *Black Poetry.* Oxford, Blackwell.

Goodman, Y. (1986). Children coming to know literacy. In Jager Adams, M. (ed.), *Beginning to Read.* Cambridge, MA, MIT Press.

Goswami, U. and Bryant, P. (1991). *Phonological Skills and Learning to Read.* Hove, Lawrence Erlbaum Associates.

Hannon, P., Jackson, A. and Weinburger, J. (1986). Parents' and teachers' strategies in hearing young children read. *Research Papers in Education, 1*(1), 6–25.

Harding, D.W. (1977) What happens when we read? In Meek, M. *et al.* (eds), *The Cool Web: The Pattern of Children's Reading.* London, The Bodley Head.

Harrison, G. (1979). 'Alone in the Grange'. In *A First Poetry Book.* Oxford, Oxford University Press.

Hasan, R. (1989). *Linguistics, Language and Verbal Art.* Oxford, Oxford University Press.

Hopkins, G.M. (1881). 'Inversnaid'. In Gardner, W.H. (ed.) (1953), *Gerard Manley Hopkins' Poems and Prose.* Harmondsworth, Penguin.

Hughes, T. (1957). 'Wind'. In *The Hawk in the Rain.* London, Faber and Faber.

Hunt, P. (1991). *Criticism, Theory and Children's Literature.* Oxford, Blackwell.

International Association for the Evaluation of Educational Achievement (1993). *How in the World Do Students Read? Times Educational Supplement.*

Iser, W. (1972). The reading process: A phenomenological approach. In Lodge, D. (ed.) (1988), *Modern Criticism and Theory.* London, Longman.

Iser, W. (1978). *The Act of Reading.* Baltimore, MD, Johns Hopkins University Press.

Ishiguro, K. (1989). *The Remains of the Day.* London, Faber and Faber.

Kemp, G. (1979). *The Turbulent Term of Tyke Tyler.* London, Puffin.

Koestler, A. (1964). *The Act of Creation.* London, Hutchinson.

Line, D. (1970). *Run for Your Life.* Harmondsworth, Puffin.

Lodge, D. (1977). *The Modes of Modern Writing.* London, Arnold.

MacMonagle, N. (ed.) (1993). *Lifelines: Letters from Famous People about their Poems.* Dublin, Town House.

Meek, M. (1983). How do they know it's worth it? In Arnold, R. (ed.), *Timely Voices.* Oxford, Oxford University Press.

Meek, M. (1988). *How Texts Teach What Readers Learn.* Lockwood, Thimble Press.

Merrick, B. (1993). Magic stones: Poems in the primary classroom. *Reading, 27*(1), 31–34.

126   *Readers and texts in the primary years*

Merrick, B. and Balaam, J. (1990). *Poetry 5–8.* Sheffield, NATE.
Minns, H. (1990). *Read It To Me Now.* London, Virago.
Murphy, J. (1978). *The Worst Witch.* Harmondsworth, Puffin.
National Curriculum: English (1994). London, HMSO.
Pearce, P. (1985). *The Way to Sattin Shore.* London, Puffin.
Perara, K. (1984). *Children's Writing and Reading: Analysing Classroom Language.* Oxford, Blackwell.
Perara, K. (1993). The good book: linguistic aspects. In Beard, R. (ed.), *Teaching Literacy: Balancing Perspectives.* London, Hodder and Stoughton.
Protherough, R. (1983). *Developing Response to Fiction.* Milton Keynes, Open University Press.
Pumfrey, P. and Reason, R. (1991). *Specific Learning Difficulties (Dyslexia),* London, NFER and Nelson.
Rimmon-Keenan, S. (1983). *Narrative Fiction: Contemporary Poetics.* London, Methuen.
Scott, A. (1993). *The Blyton phenomenon. Language and Learning* (March 1993), pp. 32–35.
Selden, R. (1989). *Practising Theory and Reading Literature.* Brighton, Harvester Wheatsheaf.
Sendak, M. (1967). Where the Wild Things Are. London, Bodley Head.
Smith, F. (1988). *Joining the Literacy Club.* London, Heinemann.
Stephens, J. (1992). *Language and Ideology in Children's Fiction.* London, Longman.
Stibbs, A. (1993). The teacherly practice of literary theory. *English in Education,* 27(2) 50–58.
Thorne, J. (1989). What is a poem? In Van Peer, W. (ed.), *The Taming of the Text.* London, Routledge.
Tolkien, J.R.R. (1964). *Tree and Leaf.* London, Allen and Unwin.
Townsend, S. (1982). *The Secret Diary of Adrian Mole Aged 13¾.* London, Methuen.
Tucker, N. (1981). *The Child and the Book,* Cambridge, Cambridge University Press.
Wells, G. (1986). *The Meaning Makers.* London, Heinemann.
Wright, K. (1985). 'The Frozen Man'. In *Golden Apples.* London, Heinemann.

Index

DEVELOPING READERS IN THE MIDDLE YEARS

Elaine Millard

Are there developmental stages in reading response? Can these be promoted or accelerated by classroom experience? The debate about standards in reading has largely ignored such questions and focused on the methods used to introduce children to print in the early years of school. Less attention has been given to ways of nurturing the habit once the first stages are past. Elaine Millard explores how assumptions about what is pleasurable in reading set an agenda for the middle years which ignores crucial differences in children's reading habits, particularly those related to gender. She argues that the more advanced reading skills of analysis, evaluation and critical response can be introduced to children at this stage but that they require the support of a classroom context that encourages co-operation and which builds on shared habits of reading.

Contents
Introduction – Section One: Reading as a social contract – Learning to read and its legacy – the pleasures of reading examined – Building communities of readers – Readers into writers – Reading: A question of gender? Section Two. Putting principles to work – Reading and writing stories together – Making good use of information books – How should children's reading be assessed? – References – Index.

176pp   0 335 19071 5 (Paperback)

THE PRIMARY LANGUAGE BOOK (Second edition)

Peter Dougill

Language coordinators in primary and middle schools must not only possess a considerable range of expertise across the language curriculum but must also be able to assist their colleagues to develop classroom practice.

In this updated and expanded revision of the successful first edition, *The Primary Language Book* examines how primary teachers can tackle the problems linked to the design and implementation of school language policies. They look in particular at:

- talking and listening
- the writing process
- reading
- media and drama
- microcomputers and language development
- knowledge about language
- liaison and continuity, and
- managing curriculum change.

Contents

144pp   0 335 190219 (Paperback)

READING AGAINST RACISM

Emrys Evans (ed.)

Reading Against Racism addresses the reading and teaching of literature and its relationship to differences of race and culture in English-speaking countries. It assumes that literature in English should be drawn from different cultures and countries in order to foster in readers self-knowledge and awareness of cultural diversity. Practically oriented, it recommends and discusses the classroom use of novels, poems and plays written in the Indian subcontinent, South Africa, the Caribbean, the USA and other countries. Drawing upon a number of different traditions, and coming from a number of different countries and backgrounds, the contributors show how reading literature can be a basic plank in anti-racist education. As Anthony Adams writes in his introduction: 'In its consistent advocacy of a positive approach to the challenge of anti-racist education and its celebration of the role of literature in this context, it breaks new ground in its thinking and provides a beginning for committed classroom work.'

Contents
Introduction – Part 1: Contexts – Language against racism in the UK: the classroom as a multilingual publishing house – Children's books in a multicultural world: a view from the USA – Reading against racism in South Africa – Mirror and springboard: an Australian teacher grows up – Part 2: Case studies – Journey to Jo'burg: reading a novel with years 7 and 8 – In at the deep end: English and Bengali verse – 'Can you fully understand it?': approaching issues of racism with white students in the English classroom – The use of literature in the ESL classroom – A year 10 story writing project – Widening the field: new literature for older students – Bringing the writer in from the cold – Books for use in the classroom – The teacher' bookshelf – Index.

Contributors
Napheas Akhter, Rudine Sims Bishop, Emrys Evans, Jim Kable, Shahana Mirza, Beverley Naidoo, Denise Newfield, Sibani Raychaudhuri, Lena Strang.

176pp   0 335 09544 5 (Paperback)